Catch
the

EXPERIENCE THE
THRILL OF SPIRIT-
EMPOWERED
LIVING!

Catch the

Wave

EXPERIENCE THE
THRILL OF SPIRIT-
EMPOWERED
LIVING!

STEVEN COLE

CREATION
HOUSE PRESS

CATCH THE WAVE by Steven Cole
Published by Creation House Press
A part of Strang Communications Company
600 Rinehart Road
Lake Mary, Florida 32746
www.creationhouse.com

Unless otherwise noted, all Scripture quotations are from the Holy Bible, New International Version. Copyright © 1973, 1978, 1984, International Bible Society. Used by permission.

Scripture quotations marked KJV are from the King James Version of the Bible.

Cover design by Karen Gonsalves

Library of Congress Catalog Card Number: 2003103161
International Standard Book Number: 1-59185-223-4

03 04 05 06 — 87654321
Printed in the United States of America

This book is dedicated to all of us as we joyfully align ourselves to our Savior and to His work.

Contents

Foreword ix

Preface xi

Introduction .xiii

1 My Story 1

2 Anatomy of a Miracle 11

3 The Holy Spirit Baptism 27

4 The Gifts of the Spirit 47

5 Spiritual Warfare 67

6 Hearing God's Voice 77

Notes 89

Foreword

There is only a handful of lay people to whom I hand the microphone during our worship services at Faith Community Church. Steven Cole is one of them. I know that I can trust him to bring a fresh, timely and sensitive word from the Lord. He hears from God and is gifted to bring forth the message in a relaxed manner that results in both blessing and edification.

Learning to minister accurately in the power of the Holy Spirit without becoming trivial, weird or spooky is a challenge for every believer who desires to fulfill his or her God-given destiny. For years, Steven has offered his *Catch the Wave Seminar* to our congregation, helping many Christians do just that. Now, by putting the practical information in book form, many more can learn how to hear from God and respond to His voice. I know I have heard His voice speaking through Steven, and I believe *you* too will hear his voice as you read this book.

—Dr. Jim Reeve
Faith Community Church

Preface

One of the mysteries of Christianity is how one God can be represented in three distinct personalities: Father, Son and Holy Spirit. Theologians call it the Trinity, but the biblical term is "the Godhead." The personalities of God are always in harmony with one another. Each has His own responsibilities. The Father is the Master Architect of the universe. The Son is Creator and Redeemer. The Holy Spirit is the Implementer of the will of each person of the Godhead. He is God's presence we sense, God's voice we hear and God's power on earth. The Holy Spirit is God's seal on our hearts and lives. (See 2 Corinthians 1:22; Ephesians 1:13.)

The Holy Spirit is largely ignored in much of the church today. We ask people to "invite Jesus into your heart" even though Jesus is at the right hand of the Father (Rom. 8:34; Heb. 12:2). What we are really doing is encouraging people to accept the sovereignty of the Father (Christ was made Lord; lordship is generally associated with the second person of the Trinity), the salvation purchased by Jesus and the presence and guidance of the Holy Spirit. God understands what we mean and accepts us where we are. Praise God! The better we understand and use proper terminology, however, the less we are confused by the Scriptures.

The purpose of this book is to aid in that process. I want to help the church understand and think properly about the role of the Holy Spirit in the life of the Spirit-filled believer. Too often the baptism in the Holy Spirit is seen as just an entry into the inner circle of a Pentecostal church.

Real ministry is left to the paid staff or the select few who prophesy on Sunday morning. If there is a main point to this book, it is be "You can minister, too." Jesus intended that each member of His church be led by the Holy Spirit in some level of ministry. I hope this book will encourage every reader to step beyond his current comfort level and get involved in touching people with the power of the Spirit.

Many books on the baptism of the Holy Spirit or on spiritual gifts go beyond what the Bible actually says. I do not want to do that. The only reliable information we have on the subject is in the Word of God. Going beyond the Bible has the potential to teach false doctrine, to leave a false impression of what God wants for each of us. It would be better not to teach anything than to leave the reader with a false impression or attitude toward God. Where personal experiences are mentioned, they elaborate and illustrate what the Scripture says, but the Scripture is foremost in this book.

Introduction

In the history of religion the Hebrews were unique. All the other societies had multiple gods. They had a god for everything. The sun was a god, the moon was a god, trees were gods, animals were gods, and even rocks were gods. These gods were much like the people who worshiped them. They ate, drank and got drunk. They slept and became angry. At times they acted foolishly. They had sexual relations with one another and occasionally with ordinary humans, creating demi-gods.

The God of the Hebrews is not like mankind at all. The God of the Hebrews is a God of extremes. He always loves, always acts with great wisdom, always does right, is always vigilant. There is no being more powerful or with more knowledge or wisdom. He is not confined to a specific location. He is everywhere, but separate from the physical world. He is beyond our comprehension. In fact, one of the arguments for the existence of God is His dissimilarity to mankind. If God really exists, it is reasoned, He must be of a different nature than mankind, not just a copy of man with special powers.

Throughout the Old Testament, God identifies Himself as one of a kind. All the other gods and idols worshiped by other societies are just created things. The main purpose of the plagues in Egypt was to show that God had power over all the gods worshiped by the Egyptians.

The New Testament reveals that the one God of the Hebrews appears in three personalities, which are called the

Godhead in Scripture.[1] God the Father is the Master Architect of the universe. God the Son is Jesus, our Savior. God the Holy Spirit leads us to salvation through conviction, conveys the felt presence of God to us, and leads and instructs us as we live our lives. He is the Comforter Jesus promised to leave with us before He ascended to God the Father.[2] Finally, the Holy Spirit is the power of God on the earth.

This book deals at length with the Holy Spirit, the least understood member of the Godhead. Many churches completely ignore Him or acknowledge Him only in passing. As we read the Book of Acts in the Bible, we see the Holy Spirit constantly at work: speaking through prophecy, acting in power to strike Ananias and Sapphira dead, healing and raising people from the dead. As dramatic as these events are, He also works behind the scenes in the hearts of tens of thousands as the Gospel spreads throughout the known world. The miraculous work of the Holy Spirit is primarily to facilitate His work in the heart of man. Miracles are transitory; His work in men's hearts is eternal.

Throughout history there have been periods when the Holy Spirit was especially active. We call them revivals. These have occurred about every twenty to forty years. His activities are like waves on the ocean. Sadly, however, believers easily miss these periods of the Holy Spirit's activity. The purpose of this book is to help the reader be aware of the Holy Spirit's activity and to partner with Him—to catch the wave of the Holy Spirit.

Chapter One

My Story

I was born on December 6, 1948 at Queen of Angels Hospital. My father was a hardworking man who had left high school at the age of seventeen to join the Merchant Marines during World War II. By the age of twenty, he had been around the world twice. He left the sea to marry my mother a year before I was born. My mother became a "housewife" upon marrying and was always there for my younger brother and me. We were a middle-class family living a middle-class life.

My mother was a believer, and my father claimed to be, but we did not attend church. They moved from South Central Los Angeles to the suburbs of Azusa in 1955. After the move, they were unable to find a church in which they felt comfortable. I attended church on a few occasions, but it made no real impression on my life.

My first real contact with God was when I was eleven. I was joining the Boy Scouts and had to memorize the Scout Oath and Law. I was having trouble with it, so I prayed that

God would help me. He did, and for the first time I realized that the stuff I had heard in those few Sunday school classes was true and that God was real.

I grew up as a "good kid," but I was chubby, uncoordinated and wore glasses. In addition to this, I am dyslexic. I didn't learn to read until the seventh grade. These all combined to make me a target for abuse by other kids throughout elementary and junior high school. These things made two impacts upon my life: First, I became a loner. At least by sticking to myself with few friends I stayed away from those most set on tormenting me. Second, I used my intellect to create verbal darts I would hurl at anyone who threatened to get too close. The combination worked most of the time; but that, combined with a naturally quiet and thoughtful nature, gave me a morose and sullen personality.

By the time I reached high school I was definitely a member of the "out" crowd and didn't like it. Starting college in 1966, I decided to change my image no matter what it cost. The best way seemed to be to join a club. The clubs on campus introduced themselves to new students during a week early in the fall semester. Booths were set up in the student center. The day I showed up to look for a club, the only booth that was manned was for a nondenominational Christian club called Alpha-Omega. I figured that I was already a Christian, so I decided to try it out.

As I started going to the club meetings, the president of the club, and probably every other member, saw my need for the Savior. The president of AΩ invited me to his church. I thought, *If you really want to find out what the church is like, go to the evening service.* So I did. The evening I showed up, the Teen Challenge choir was "performing" at the church. (Teen Challenge is an organization that works with drug addicts helping them become free from drugs and find a new life in Christ.) I still remember one testimony. The speaker had been arrested and convicted for possession of drugs. He was on bail before sentencing when he was introduced to Jesus Christ through Teen Challenge. His life was obviously changed by the Savior. I wanted what this drug addict had discovered. When the altar call was given, I went forward. I expected over half the church to join me, but I was the only one. The pastor tried to talk to me later that evening, but I was so overwhelmed by the experience I could do nothing but bawl. My life had changed in an evening!

I started reading the New Testament every spare moment I found. I was growing fast. A couple of months later I decided to return to my high school and share what I had discovered with my favorite teacher. That was one of the hardest things I have ever done. He, for all I could tell, was a hard-nosed, intellectual agnostic and did not want to hear about some kid's epiphany. He was polite, but not much more.

A few weeks after that experience I was invited to an evening home prayer meeting. When I arrived, I soon found that this was not just another prayer meeting. The host, John Baker, was teaching about something called the baptism in the Holy Spirit. He said it would give believers power to share their faith. I immediately thought of that encounter with my high school teacher. I wanted what John had. At the end of the meeting, a few asked for prayer. John, along with others, prayed for them one by one. All the while an argument was going on between me and "the Voice" that I knew was God. He wanted me to ask for prayer, and I was not that sure I wanted to. About the time I gave in to the urging of God, John was talking to a young man just behind my chair. I waited for an opportunity to interrupt, and I asked John to pray for me. He encouraged me to give voice to whatever sounds were going through my mind, and I did. When I finally got up, I could barely walk. I understood why the disciples on the Day of Pentecost were accused of being drunk. I was "drunk in the Spirit." This was the second experience that changed my life.

I had always been a thinker. When I was fifteen, I had almost convinced myself that there was no physical reality and I was a disembodied brain being fed impulses in a jar somewhere. I needed something more than just theology to hold on to my faith. God knew that, and He gave me the baptism in the Holy Spirit. It is His involvement in my life that continually convinces me of the reality of God.

At that time I attended an American Baptist Church in Azusa. Our pastor, Frank Mason, was a white South African who had become an American citizen. He and others invited me to a Charismatic prayer meeting held in a nearby house after the Sunday evening service. The first time I attended was the Sunday before my experience at the Baker's. I noticed some of the people speaking in a language other than English, but since Pastor Mason was South African, I assumed it was he and maybe others who shared his heritage. As I attended the next week, after being filled with the Holy Spirit, I realized they were speaking in tongues as I was. That evening, as I prayed for people, I prayed in my new language. Then God gave me words in English, and I spoke them. I alternately prayed in tongues and spoke the words God gave me for most of the evening. As I continued attending the meetings, I learned about the gifts of the Spirit and saw them demonstrated.

One evening a woman in a wheelchair came to the meeting and asked for prayer. She was dying from some illness and had only weeks to live. She was not asking for healing. She had a larger problem. Her husband had either died or left her, and she had no one to take care of her children. She was almost frantic trying to find someone in time for her children to get to know them before her death. We prayed. We felt nothing special, but God moved. A few weeks later we heard the news she had been completely healed, giving her doctors a real problem. Most requests we prayed for were not nearly that dramatic, but every week we heard reports of how God moved.

After I had been going to such meetings for a year or so, David Sweet came to the meeting, and I felt drawn to him. He had an interest in electronics, and I was studying to be an electronics technician. We became fast friends. I didn't know it at the time, but he had just come to Jesus as Savior. A few years before he had been a white witch. Over the next few years he gradually told me bits and pieces of the things he was involved in prior to his conversion. He was a short man and routinely got beat up as a kid. He wanted power; Satan gave it to him. He started hearing the thoughts of those around him. Soon the continual buzz of the thoughts of others in his mind drove him to drink. By the age of twenty he was an alcoholic. He found that if he reached for a pack of cigarettes, an invisible force would make them slide into his hand. He could control the path of a billiard ball or the shape of a candle flame by his mind. He was a white witch and thought he was serving God with these powers, but he had no peace. David was gradually getting out of it when he met and married his wife. She led him to church where he met Jesus and found the peace he needed.

When David came to Jesus as Savior, God almost instantly gave him a depth in the Holy Spirit equal to the depth he had experienced in Satan. This was frightening to many in our church, but between the church's solid teaching and reading the Bible for himself, David had a solid foundation for his new Christian life. He enrolled in Azusa Pacific College (now Azusa Pacific University) and soon started a Charismatic teaching meeting at his house. I was part of the group who attended regularly.

I started teaching now and then in David's house meeting. One evening as I was teaching, David asked, "Where does the Bible say that?" It was as if someone slapped me on the side of my head. I realized that the Bible didn't say that. What I was teaching may have been true from experience, but without a biblical foundation for my teaching, it could easily have given the wrong impression. That small question has never left me. Whatever I teach now, I feel constrained to make sure that, somewhere, the Bible does say that!

At about the same time I got involved in a group meeting in the home of a married couple living on campus at Azusa Pacific College. One summer, the host of the group became involved in a Salvation Army summer camp. Others from the group and I were hired as staff members. While this was going on, I had started prophesying to myself during my personal prayer time. I thought I was hearing the voice of God. I was convinced that I would marry shortly after the summer and join the group leader in Arizona on a ranch he was dreaming of starting. Nothing worked out as I expected. I learned through this experience to verify what I think is God by two or three witnesses before jumping into free space "in faith." I am still not sure where that "direction" came from—my own desires or Satan—but I know it wasn't God.

I went back to school, and after graduating in 1969, I became an electronics technician. After working for about a year, I moved out of my parents' house and into my own apartment. I was working for a company that made instrumentation tape recorders used by NASA. At the end of the Apollo program, companies like the one I worked for had to lay off many workers because NASA no longer needed their products. Sure enough, I was out of work. The slump in technical industries was so great that Ph.D.'s were pumping gas. The week after I was laid off, a couple from our church was raising support to go to Brazil as music-missionaries. I heard what I knew to be God's voice tell me to give $100 of the $530 I had received as severance pay. I tried to tell God how I needed all the money I had, but He promised me that if I trusted Him and obeyed, He would take care of me. I gulped and wrote a check. I was out of work for six weeks. When I started work again and received the first check, I had about $23 in the bank. I never missed a meal, a rent payment or a car payment, nor did I have to plead for help from my parents. I learned that God is faithful as long as I obey.

By the age of twenty-five I had been praying for a wife for a long time. My mother saw an advertisement in the local paper for a Christian group that met at Clifton's Cafeteria on Sunday mornings. She gave me the ad and encouraged me to go.

Unknown to me, Mrs. Dorothy Rahn was encouraging her daughter, Linda, to go to the same meeting. We both showed up for the first time on the same day. I saw her come in and thought, *Wow, she looks promising!* She was thinking, *He is good-looking. I wonder if he knows the Scriptures?* She watched me through that first meeting. On subsequent meetings and at lunch with the group I always managed to sit next to her. I tried to impress her with how quickly I could find a reference in my Bible as I asked gently probing questions: "Are you working? For how long? Where do you attend church? What do you think about…?" I was shy. She wondered why I didn't ask her out. I was scared stiff! I finally asked her to church (safe), and she agreed. We saw each other three times that week. By the following Sunday, I was saying things like, "After we get married..." to see the reaction I would get. If she caught the reference to marriage, she didn't react but took my comment in stride. During the following week I made it official and asked her to marry me.

Linda was attending a Plymouth Brethren church. The denomination was dead-set against the Charismatic Movement and all it implied, especially tongues! I had been prophesied over a number of times at a number of different meetings that God would give me a nationwide ministry if I would follow and obey Him. I knew that it involved teaching on the baptism in the Holy Spirit. I needed a wife who would support me in this ministry. I decided to take her to one of the Charismatic meetings at David Sweet's house. I had been attending there regularly for several years, but this would be Linda's first exposure to a Charismatic meeting. Robbie, a woman regularly at the meeting, flowed in the word of knowledge. She read Linda just as Jesus did with the woman at the well. Then, Robbie and Alene, David's wife, started giggling. They knew that Linda would end up as my wife, but Linda had no idea what the joke was. All this scared Linda, but she watched Robbie's eyes and saw them as trustworthy. In the car after the meeting I explained what had happened and how it worked. When she got home, she checked it out in the Bible for herself. She knew that if it was in the Bible, it was God's plan, even if her church didn't teach it. The Bible settled it in her mind. We were married on August 11, 1973, just three months after our first official date.

Shortly after getting married I went to work as an engineering technician at Conrac in Duarte, California, making television monitors for military systems. While there, I came to truly understand how electronic circuitry worked. After two years, I was doing junior engineer level work. Because I only had an associate degree, they refused to give me the title or the pay at a level I felt I deserved; therefore, I left. Through the aid of a professional placement agency commonly called a "headhunter," I got a job as an engineer at Omnus Computer in Anaheim. I continued to hone my engineering skills. I went to work for the Jet Propulsion Laboratory when Omnus folded about two and one-half years later. JPL hired me as a junior engineer since I had come from a small company where titles are easy to come by. After about a year on the job, I was promoted to full engineer. I have now been working for JPL for over twenty years. I am a well-respected senior engineer specializing in developing instrumentation systems for ground support of spacecraft. I have applied the same attention to detail and an innovative approach to the Word of God that enabled me to become a senior engineer even without a four-year college degree.

Linda and I have two children. Our oldest, James, was born with one fist raised to the world. James has always loved God, but although he has mellowed in recent years, he has always been a handful. When James started to go through puberty, he started having problems with his body. He would be talking to you and then suddenly blank out, suffering what is called a petit mal seizure. The doctors finally diagnosed five different kinds of epileptic seizures and started him on medication. James was allergic to all the preferred medications. What they finally had him on made him somewhat catatonic but did not stop the seizures, which were numbering between five and twelve per day. The process to get to this point took over a year from the initial diagnosis. Linda and I were praying for him every day. We saw no improvement, but we continued to trust God for James' healing. From time to time, we were given the usual advice—if we just pray more and believe, God would heal James. But God had His timing.

James had always been a control freak. Now, the control he valued most—control of his own body—was denied him. The battle raging within James was not medical but spiritual. Would he yield to God's control? When he finally did, James was healed. We were attending an evening service one Sunday, and the pastor invited those seeking healing to come forward. That day James had his usual count of seizures. He went forward, received prayer and has never had another seizure to this day.

Jonathan was a much more compliant child. He was very receptive to God and accepted Jesus as his Savior when he was around two years old. Although he had a speech problem and was severely dyslexic, he often scared Linda by wandering off, going up to total strangers and asking them if they knew Jesus as their Savior. Jon's speech problem was cured by therapy. His reading problems have not been healed, but through learning phonics, he was able to read at or near grade level all through school. He is now in a pastoral internship program.

A few years ago, after a number of false starts, I held the first "Catch the Wave Seminar on the Holy Spirit." I combined a teaching on the gifts of the Holy Spirit with a few other teachings I have created over the years, and the seminar was born. It was well received and continued to be over the next three years. We have often had people attend more than once, saying that there was so much information communicated that it was hard to get it all in one sitting. I have refined it, but it has largely remained unchanged. I have placed the information—and more than I could possibly teach in a seminar—in this book.

Chapter Two

Anatomy of a Miracle

A man had a flat tire. He stopped to fix it next to a chain link fence. On the other side of the fence was an insane asylum. As he worked to change the tire, an inmate watched. The man took the lug nuts off and placed them in the hubcap. But when he pulled the tire from the car, it hit the hubcap and the lug nuts went flying. They landed in the storm drain, out of reach. Puzzled about what to do, the man stared at the car for a long moment.

Then the inmate spoke up. "Why don't you take one lug nut from each of the other three wheels? That should get you to the nearest auto supply store where you can buy more." Astonished, the man now stared at the inmate. In response to his stare, the inmate added, "I'm here because I'm crazy, not stupid!"

That's an old joke, but our assumptions about what to expect from someone can color our interaction with that person. This is never more true than with Jesus. We acknowledge Him to be part of the Trinity. As such, when

He performs miracles, our natural response is, "Of course; after all, He is God." We tend to look at the incarnate Jesus as God with a thin covering of skin. We see Him as not really human; just pretending to be human for our sake.

But we have a problem. In John 14:12 Jesus said, "I tell you the truth, anyone who has faith in me will do what I have been doing. He will do even greater things than these, because I am going to the Father." If Jesus does miracles because He is God, how can we do greater miracles than He did since we are fully human? Obviously, there is something wrong with our assumptions. Let's take a few minutes to examine just how the incarnate Jesus functioned.

Jesus As a Role Model

In Philippians 2:6–7, Paul tells us that Jesus "made himself nothing." Literally, the Greek word used here, *kenoo*, means "to make empty." Jesus emptied Himself of divine power and became human. On earth He functioned as a human—sinless and perfect, in perfect relationship with His Father, but human.

We can see this in Satan's attack on Jesus. In Matthew 4:1–11, the Holy Spirit led Jesus into the wilderness after Jesus had been baptized by John. After the forty-day fast, Satan came. He said to Jesus, "If you are the Son of God, tell these stones to become bread."[1]

Satan started the attack by tempting Jesus to doubt His origin and Person by saying, "*If* you *are* the Son of God…" Satan knew who Jesus was. He hoped to cast doubt in Jesus' own mind as to His origin. Satan wanted Jesus to act using His power as a member of the Godhead. Satan hoped that Jesus would do this, not just to create bread, but also to prove that He was who He claimed to be. Jesus could have created anything He chose. After all, He spoke worlds into existence. It would have been no problem for Him to take a stone and, "poof," bread, or even, "poof," a bagel with cream cheese. To do that, however, He would have to act as God. He would be acting apart from the will of the Father and apart from His role as perfect man. That was Satan's ultimate goal: to separate the Son from the Father. Needless to say, Satan did not succeed.

Jesus needed to be the first truly obedient human being if He was to take the place that Adam lost in the Fall of man in the Garden of Eden. Paul refers to Jesus as the second (or last) Adam in 1 Corinthians 15:45–49. The first Adam failed through sin, but the last Adam didn't.

After Adam's creation, God intended him to grow slowly in wisdom and knowledge. God's plan was for man to rule creation in partnership with God, but Adam chose a faster and easier path, forever losing his destiny as well as ours. Jesus came to recapture it. He came to buy it back with His very blood. Jesus became human because only a human being could restore man to a perfect relationship with God. Only a human Jesus could restore man to the shared leadership role God originally intended. Isaiah 59:15–17 says:

> Truth is nowhere to be found, and whoever shuns evil becomes a prey. The LORD looked and was displeased that there was no justice. He saw that there was no one, he was appalled that there was no one to intervene; so his own arm worked salvation for him, and his own righteousness sustained him. He put on righteousness as his breastplate, and the helmet of salvation on his head; he put on the garments of vengeance and wrapped himself in zeal as in a cloak.

Jesus didn't perform miracles because He was God with skin on. Rather, He performed miracles while functioning as a human being. Therefore, Jesus Himself was the model for us, showing us how to fulfill His promise of John 14:12: "I tell you the truth, anyone who has faith in me will do what I have been doing. He will do even greater things than these, because I am going to the Father."

Jesus tells us how in John 5:1–20.

THE OUTWARD VIEW—
THE POOL OF BETHESDA

In this story, Jesus was in Jerusalem for a feast. As He approached the temple, He passed the pool of Bethesda. This was actually two square pools placed side by side. A covered walkway surrounded and separated them. From above they would look like a squared number 8. The lame, crippled and blind surrounded the pools, lying under the covering. They were waiting for the waters to be troubled by an angel. To this day we don't know if the story of the water troubling was just a folk story or a real miracle that occurred from time to time. However, it is hard to believe that so many would be just lying there if the story had not been true. Whether it was true or not, those who were there were looking for and awaiting healing.

Jesus must have passed the pool many times before as He went back and forth to the temple. This time His eye fell on a particular man. Jesus knew that he had been ill for thirty-eight years. We don't know how He knew. Perhaps someone told Him, or it was a word of knowledge from the Holy Spirit. In any case, Jesus started a dialogue with him: "Do you want to get well?"[2]

To us, this seems to be a stupid question. In his culture,

however, a lame man could earn a living being a beggar. He would lose his income if he were healed. He had probably not learned a trade if he had been lame from childhood. Being healed would lead to poverty—at least until he could learn a trade.

Today, Jesus may ask us, "Are you willing to lose your excuse for sympathy?" We no longer allow those with some infirmity to beg in the streets as they did in that era. Often, however, our illness or infirmity becomes so much a part of who we are that, to tell the truth, we don't want to get well. We would rather remain in our condition than be challenged to grow beyond our condition. To be healed we must change. Change would involve doing what we have never done. That can be very frightening!

In response to Jesus, the man said, "Sir, I have no one to help me into the pool when the water is stirred. While I am trying to get in, someone else goes down ahead of me" (v. 7). In effect he is saying, "If you want to help, hang around and help me into the pool when the water is troubled." The lame man had no idea what was coming. He certainly did not look to Jesus as a healer.

Jesus commanded the man to take up his mat and walk. Instantly, a miracle of healing happened as the man's legs received the strength to be able to do as Jesus commanded. I wish I could have watched his face as suddenly he realized that he wasn't lame anymore. The now-healed man obeyed Jesus and walked off without even learning Jesus' name.

We are conditioned to pray for God to act. But Jesus trained His disciples in a different way. He told His disciples to *speak* words in faith to accomplish miracles. Jesus taught in Matthew 17:20, "I tell you the truth, if you have faith as small as a mustard seed, you can say to this mountain,

'Move from here to there' and it will move. Nothing will be impossible for you."

Each miracle Jesus performed was different. He seldom prayed but often spoke miracles into existence, just as He spoke worlds into existence thousands of years before. He spoke to storms, and they were calmed. He spoke to the dead, and they came to life. He healed the lame, diseased and blind with *spoken* words.

Jesus taught that *our* words could have power as well. For God to act based on our words, our words must be under control. If we curse or use Jesus' name in other than a respectful way, God cannot invest our words with power. Imagine what would happen if every time a believer said, "God damn..." and He did! What if every time a believer said "Go to hell" there were a puff of smoke and the person or thing being spoken to disappeared! The more we grow in our ability to control our speech, the more we can see God act through our words.

Jesus spent many hours in prayer. He did so alone, with just Himself and the Father. He didn't wait until a miracle was needed to prepare Himself in prayer. He lived a life of prayer. If we are to do the works Jesus did, we need two things. First, we need to be prepared in prayer just as Jesus was. Second, at the point of action, we must speak to the problem rather than just praying. God already knows the problem, and He has already decided upon a course of action. If we know His will, we can speak His will into existence just as Jesus did that day. We will say more about this later.

Let us return to the scene at the pool of Bethesda. The man who was lame a few moments earlier now walked away. What would have been the natural reaction of the crowd? They were waiting for healing, and now a man among them is healed. The only plausible reaction is for each one there to beg for healing as well. The Scripture doesn't say so, but we would expect that each of them would be calling, shouting, waving his or her arms trying to get Jesus' attention. The focus of all who were there seeking healing would have turned from the pool to Jesus.

What was Jesus' response? Did He heal anyone else? No! He turned and walked away!

There were occasions when Jesus healed everyone present. Sometimes He healed everyone with a need in the whole town. This was not such a moment. We must realize that each healing and every miracle God performs are special gifts of grace! It is a precious gift of unmerited favor from our heavenly Father to one of His kids. God is under no obligation in any way to produce a miracle for us. He is not compelled to act by His Word or by our faith or because of our piety. There is no magical verse or phrase we can recite that will force God to act. There is no way to require God to perform according to our will. In fact, *we* must perform *His* will. That is why *we* call Him Lord. God has no crank on His side that says, "Turn here for a miracle." Some who came out of the "faith movement" have the impression that God is required to act in response to our faith. The problem comes when God doesn't act. What started in faith often ends in feelings of guilt for not having enough faith for the desired miracle. In reality, for His own reasons, God may choose not to act. Then, the misunderstanding of God's dealings may result in feelings of condemnation.

God has promised to do what is the very best for all those who love Him. The way He defines "best," however, is not the same way we do. He has an agenda for us as stated in Romans 8:28–29:

17

And we know that in all things God works for the
good of those who love him, who have been called
according to his purpose. For those God foreknew
he also predestined to be conformed to the likeness of his Son, that he might be the firstborn
among many brothers.

Here, God defines "good" as being "conformed to the
likeness of his Son." That is the good to which all things
work. That is why Jesus is our ultimate role model in ministry. If God can work out the image of Jesus in us and provide a healing at the same time, He will—because He loves
us. If He has to sacrifice physical healing for building the
image of Jesus in us, building Jesus' image in us comes first.

The man who had been healed at the pool of Bethesda
was confronted by the Pharisees for carrying his mat on the
Sabbath. There is nothing in the Law of Moses about carrying things on the Sabbath. The Jewish teachers had "built
a wall around the Torah." That means they made rules that
made it harder to accidentally break a Law of Moses.

For instance, the Law of Moses said that the Jews are not
allowed to cook a kid (baby goat) in its mother's milk.[3] To
keep people from breaking the law, the Jewish teachers insti-
tuted rules that did not permit drinking milk and eating any
meat in the same meal. Then a rule was added preventing
having any milk product and any meat at the same meal. As
a result, today at hotels in Israel, one can't get meat and use
margarine or butter on bread at the same meal.

The Pharisees were afraid that, by carrying his mat on the
Sabbath, the healed man might make a mark in the ground
as he put it down. The Pharisees considered that the same as
plowing, which is work, and the Law of Moses forbade work
on the Sabbath.[4]

ANATOMY OF A MIRACLE

My friend David Sweet often says, "Poor theology is a cruel taskmaster."

It's true! Poor theology lays unnecessary burdens on our lives and makes a real relationship with God more difficult. It discourages many from the pursuit of righteousness. Jesus railed time and time again against the Pharisees for just this sort of thing. He said that they tied heavy loads on the shoulders of ordinary believers but would not even lift a finger to help carry it.[5] He called them hypocrites who strain at a gnat but swallow a camel.[6] Gnats are unclean, so they should be removed from food or drink. But a camel is also unclean and should not be eaten. Jesus described a ludicrous scene in which the Pharisees meticulously strain a gnat out of their food and then swallow an entire camel. In other words, they were careful to observe the minor things in the Law but neglected the weightier principles of godliness. Their poor theology was a real stumbling block in the path of those just trying to live good lives. Their poor theology became one of Satan's most effective weapons against God's people. We must be careful, or Satan will use the same weapon against us as well.

The man who had been lame replied to the Pharisees' rebuke by saying, "The man that healed me told me to take up my bed." He probably assumed that anyone who had such a connection with God as to heal a lame man would not tell him to do something that would break the Sabbath.

The Pharisees wanted to know who this Healer was. The man didn't even know Jesus' name. Eventually they released the man who was lame. Later, Jesus again came into contact with the man in the temple. This would have been the first time the formerly lame man would have been welcome in the temple. Those with physical infirmities were not allowed to come into the temple. Imagine what it must have been for him to be inside the temple for the first time in his entire life! He was now able to be involved in temple worship rather than just hearing it from the outside.

Jesus said, "See, you are well again. Stop sinning or something worse may happen to you."[7] As usual, Jesus' eyes were on more than this present world. The man's physical condition was no lasting impediment to his everlasting life. Sin jeopardized much more than his physical life on earth. The wages of sin is death.[8] The collective sin of mankind cost Jesus His human life. Even as a believer, repeated willful sin will extract a penalty in the believer's life and his relationship with God. Continued willful sin can even cost salvation itself.[9] Man's relationship with God is much more important than his healing. Healing is temporary; relationship with God is eternal!

The man left the temple knowing now that it was Jesus who had healed him. He went straight to the Pharisees and told them.

At their next opportunity, the Pharisees confronted Jesus for healing on the Sabbath. Jesus answered them, "I tell you the truth, the Son can do nothing by himself; he can do only what he sees his Father doing."[10] Jesus Himself says that He is powerless without the Father. He did not act as "God with skin on," but as a human being. He does what He sees the Father doing. Elsewhere, Jesus says that He only says what His Father commands Him to say.[11] He cooperates with the other members of the Godhead to bring a miracle into existence. We can perform miracles in the same way today by cooperating with God's will.

FROM JESUS' POINT OF VIEW

Let's go back over that scene with Jesus' words to the Pharisees in mind. Let's see it from Jesus' point of view.

Jesus is on His way to the temple, and the Holy Spirit taps Him on the shoulder: "See that guy, third from the left in back? The Father wants to heal him. Start a conversation." So Jesus comes right to the point, "Do you want to get well?"

In essence, the lame man replies, "Hang around so that when the water is troubled, you can help me in."

The Holy Spirit now says, "Tell him to rise, take up his bed and walk." When Jesus speaks the words, trusting the Father to act, the lame man is instantly healed.

As the formerly lame man walks away, the scene erupts in confusion as everyone else at the pool calls for healing, too. Jesus asks the Father if He wants to heal anyone else. The answer returns, "No." Jesus turns and walks off.

Only three things are required for a miracle: a need, God's willingness and a human to speak the miracle into existence. God has chosen to partner with us. Unless we choose to cooperate with God, He will not act. We will discuss this in more detail later.

SILLY LITTLE THINGS

Miracles often involve doing a silly little thing, trusting God to move, before God will act and perform a miracle. What usually stands in the way of the needed miracle is our pride. For instance, Jesus once healed a blind man by spitting in the dirt and making mud, which He then applied to the man's eyes.[12] What if the Father hadn't come through with a miracle? Imagine the reaction of the crowd if the Father had not performed the miracle. Jesus would have looked like a fool to those who saw what He did. He had to be willing to risk looking like a fool.

Even though I understand the concept, this is difficult for me. I have to constantly confront my own pride. For example, God often uses me in prophecy. I can still remember one occasion when God told me that the woman behind me in church had two sons that were like two horses. If they were allowed to go wild, they would be uncontrollable. But if she harnessed them, as horses are in front of a wagon, their strength would be directed to useful purposes, and their lives would be constructive, not destructive. It was hard for me to deliver that word from God. I thought, *What if she has two daughters, or worse yet, no children at all?* I had to be willing to look like a fool to do the work God wanted me to do at that moment. She received the word with grace, but I still don't know for sure if it fit her situation.

There is another example from the Old Testament in 2 Kings 13:14–19. In this passage, Elisha is on his deathbed, and the king of Israel came to see him. God had one thing more for the prophet to do, however. God wanted His people to totally triumph over Aram. Even being ill, the prophet could be part of the victory if only the king would cooperate.

Elisha asked the king to get his bow and arrows and bring them to his bedside. Elisha put his hands on the king's hands and then told him to shoot an arrow out the window. As the arrow flew, the prophet declared, "The Lord's arrow of victory, the arrow of victory over Aram!" Through all of this, the king had no problem with performing the actions requested by the prophet.

Then Elisha told the king to strike the remaining arrows on the ground. The king started doing this, but he also must have started thinking, *Hey, I'm the king! Here I am pounding arrows into the dirt. This is stupid! How can this stupid action have any real impact on our victory?* The king stopped. Instantly the prophet conveyed God's anger. The king had stopped too soon; he had only struck the floor three times. God wanted him to strike the floor five or six times to achieve total victory over Aram. As a result of the king's lack of faith, Israel would not have complete victory. The Israelite army would only have victory on three occasions.

The king didn't realize that silly little things have power when they are done at the direction of God. The power comes from our faith expressed in doing that silly little thing. The king was more concerned with his pride than with obedience to God and what that obedience might mean. God's miracles usually involve some silly little action, done in obedience with faith. God does this not to humiliate us, but at least in part because "God opposes the proud but gives grace to the humble."[13]

HE WANTS US TO WORK THE SAME WAY

In the Gospel of John, Jesus promised us that we would perform greater works than He did. Jesus wasn't talking about preaching to larger crowds. In context, He was referring to believers doing greater miracles than He Himself performed.

> I tell you the truth, anyone who has faith in me will do what I have been doing. He will do even greater things than these, because I am going to the Father...If you love me, you will obey what I command. And I will ask the Father, and he will give you another Counselor to be with you forever—the Spirit of truth.
>
> —JOHN 14:12–17

The reason Jesus said we can perform greater miracles than He did is because the Father was going to send the Holy Spirit to direct us in Jesus' place. It is the Holy Spirit who empowers us to fulfill Jesus' promise. The voice of the Holy Spirit within us can let us know the will of the Father in any situation. Our job is to act in faith and speak the Father's will into existence.

Just imagine the power we release when we hear the voice of the Holy Spirit and obey. The Word of God tells us that if we ask anything according to the will of the Father, He hears us. If we know He hears us, we can ask anything in faith and confidence that God will do what we ask.[14] We know the will of the Father because we hear God's voice.

There are three basic requirements for God to perform a miracle:

1. The most important requirement is for God to *want* to perform a miracle. There are no magic phrases we can use to make God perform according to our will. No amount of worked-up faith will force God to act against His will. There is no corner we can back God into to force Him to do our will. We must obey His will. That's why we call Him Lord!

2. God requires *need* to perform a miracle. God only acts in response to need. He never performs fireworks or magic. Even when God performs a dramatic miracle, He does not do it in a showy or brash way. Jesus walked on water to get to the other side of the lake, not to impress His disciples. Mark 6:48 tells us that He was about to pass by His disciples.

Jesus was just going from one side of the lake to the other.

3. God requires a *willing human being* to perform a miracle. When God created human beings, he gave them control of the earth. Genesis 1:28 reads:

> God blessed them [Adam and Eve] and said to them, "Be fruitful and increase in number; fill the earth and subdue it. Rule over the fish of the sea and the birds of the air and over every living creature that moves on the ground."

God never rescinded that authority even when Adam rebelled and gave his authority to Satan. Adam did that by rebelling against God's command when he ate the forbidden fruit. Jesus came, in part, to redeem the planet from the control of the enemy. Now we can partner with God to extend His rule where we live and work. God's command issued so long ago to subdue and rule over the earth still stands. God won't violate it, even when it seems like it's for our good, because only He knows what's best for us. Without God, we can't extend His sphere of rulership on earth. But without our involvement, God won't act! The way we partner with God is to *do* what Jesus did. He listened to the Father and acted on God's Word, His revealed will.[15] As we learn to listen to God's voice, we can do the same. The result is that God's will happens: People are healed, led into salvation and matured in the kingdom of God. And God's kingdom is advanced in a multitude of ways.

Chapter Three

The Holy Spirit Baptism

What is normal for believers? I didn't ask "What is usual?" but "What is normal?" It is usual for believers to live their whole lives without making any real contribution to the body of Christ other than financial donations. It is usual for believers to be so distracted by the world that they hardly even find out what God wants for them, much less strive to fulfill their destiny. God wants "normal" for believers to be much different. Exodus 20:4–6 tells us that God refuses to allow us to worship anything except God Himself. We can't worship carved images or idols with engines and wheels. We can't bow down to goddesses of stone or on a silver screen. We can't put statues of gold or work that earns gold before Him. God needs first place in our lives—for our sakes.

God created mankind so that He could enjoy a special

27

relationship with us. He wants this relationship with us, not just for Himself, but for our sakes as well. We have been warped by sin beyond what any of us realize. The only way that warp can be removed is for God to be first and foremost in our lives. We have a need to be committed to Him. When we are fully committed, we grow in relationship with God as He slowly removes the warp from our lives. We also become increasingly involved in doing God's work here.

The baptism in the Holy Spirit is crucial in this process. The baptism allows God to speak to us and lead us more precisely. Through the baptism, a new realm opens to us; that is the realm of Spirit where God operates. God is Spirit. Human beings can only operate in the realm of flesh without God's help. To receive God's gift of the baptism in the Spirit you must believe Jeremiah 29:11, which says:

> "For I know the plans I have for you," declares the LORD, "plans to prosper you and not to harm you, plans to give you hope and a future."

The battle is over control. We think that we are in control of our lives without God. But Jesus was correct when He said that we will either serve sin or God.[1] The irony is that while we think we are free without God, we are actually slaves to sin. Usually, fear of losing "control" is what keeps us from submitting to God. When we do submit to the lordship of God, He sets us truly free. He removes the blindfold and allows us to see the deception we had been under for so long. Receiving the baptism in the Holy Spirit is a step in this submission process.

Let us examine what is involved in the baptism and what one can expect when he or she is baptized in the Holy Spirit.

WHAT IS THE BAPTISM IN THE HOLY SPIRIT?

The word *baptize* is not translated like most words in the New Testament. Rather, it is transliterated. The word in the original Greek was copied to English and retained a very similar pronunciation. In Greek the word is *baptizo* (pronounced "bap-teed-zo"), and it means "to immerse." The word is used in an ancient pickle recipe where it calls for the immersion of cucumbers in brine. The word is used in describing the process of immersing cloth in dye to color it. A sunken ship is also spoken of as baptized in the sea. In these instances, the word implies a lasting change caused by the immersion.

Every believer has a measure of the Holy Spirit. Without Him (the Holy Spirit), we would not belong to Christ. The baptism in the Holy Spirit is as much different from that as having a glass of water is different from taking a bath. It is a difference in quantity and effect.

How, then, does the Word speak about baptisms? Hebrews 6:12 refers to "instruction about baptisms." There are three baptisms spoken about in the New Testament. First, there is the baptism spoken about in 1 Corinthians 12:13, "For we were all baptized by one Spirit into one body..." Here, the person being baptized is the believer, and the one doing the baptizing is the Holy Spirit, the third person of the Godhead. In this baptism, the believer is being immersed into the body of Christ. This is salvation, the first step in a life with Christ as Savior and Lord. Salvation is also a prerequisite for being baptized in the Holy Spirit.

Usually, the second baptism that occurs in a believer's life is the baptism commanded by Jesus in Matthew 28:19: "Therefore go and make disciples of all nations, baptizing them in the name of the Father and of the Son and of the Holy Spirit." Here again the person being baptized is the believer. The person doing the baptizing is a fellow believer. The substance into which the believer is being immersed is water. This symbolizes a death and burial to the old life of sin as the believer is submerged. Then, the believer is raised out of the water, symbolizing being raised from death to a new life in Christ.

Finally, John the Baptist spoke of a third baptism in Luke 3:16: "I baptize you with water. But one more powerful than I will come...He will baptize you with the Holy Spirit and with fire." Here too the person being baptized is the believer. The person doing the baptizing is Jesus. The believer is being immersed into the Holy Spirit.

Every believer has the Holy Spirit within, whether baptized in the Holy Spirit or not. The Holy Spirit is God's seal on the believer.[2] The difference is in magnitude, like the difference between having a glass of water on a boat and the boat being sunk, or baptized in the water.

There is one baptism in the Holy Spirit, and it lasts throughout your whole life. There are, however, multiple fillings with the Holy Spirit. The initial baptism in the Holy Spirit establishes a relationship with the Spirit. This is similar to the way salvation establishes a lifelong relationship with God. However, just as our relationship with God can require periodic renewal, we can find ourselves requiring refilling from time to time.

In Acts 4, the disciples had been persecuted by the Pharisees for preaching the gospel. They were gathered together lamenting their situation and praying:

> "Now, Lord, consider their threats and enable your
> servants to speak your word with great boldness.

Stretch out your hand to heal and perform miraculous signs and wonders through the name of Your holy servant Jesus." After they prayed, the place where they were meeting was shaken. And they were all filled with the Holy Spirit and spoke the Word of God boldly.

—ACTS 4:29–31

Those people present at that time were also present in the upper room when the Holy Spirit initially fell and baptized the disciples. Here, the disciples were not re-baptized in the Spirit, but they were refilled.

Periodic fillings are required from time to time because, as much as we try to stay filled, we *leak*. This takes place in two ways. First, the gifts of the Holy Spirit can atrophy if not used regularly. There are seasons when things flow hot and heavy. At other seasons, the Spirit doesn't *seem* to move at all. Such times make staying filled more difficult.

Second, we can offend the Spirit by refusing His leading or prompting in ministry. No matter what the times or seasons we go through as believers, God is always faithful. He wants us to be faithful, too. When we have offended the Holy Spirit in this way, we need to repent. Until we do, the Spirit will often refuse to offer us a new gift to deliver.

One thing that should be pointed out is that the Holy Spirit is unpredictable to a great extent. One can never say, "The Holy Spirit will never..." or "The Holy Spirit always..." As soon as one does, the Spirit will refuse to play by those rules. We can only express what we have seen as His normal operation. But in so doing, the reader must understand that God is inscrutable, beyond total understanding.

JESUS TELLS US THE IMPORTANCE OF THIS BAPTISM

Some believers think that the baptism is either not very important or that it occurs as an automatic part of salvation. According to the words of Jesus, He thought the baptism in the Holy Spirit was very important. Jesus had been crucified, died an atoning death, been buried and raised from the dead. One would expect Jesus to meet with His disciples and say, "OK, boys, go out and preach the good news about what I have completed." Instead, however, Jesus says, "Do not leave Jerusalem, but wait for the gift my Father promised, which you have heard me speak about. For John baptized with water, but in a few days you will be baptized with the Holy Spirit…You will receive power when the Holy Spirit comes on you; and you will be my witnesses in Jerusalem, and in all Judea and Samaria, and to the ends of the earth."[3]

The disciples were saved when, after Jesus' resurrection, He breathed on His disciples and said, "Receive the Holy Spirit."[4] At this time, they received only a measure of the Holy Spirit, because without that measure of the Spirit, one can not be truly saved.[5] Jesus was promising more than just salvation. He was talking about the power necessary to fulfill the Great Commission. Jesus knew that they needed power they didn't have. They needed the power of the Holy Spirit that was conveyed by the baptism in the Holy Spirit.

The word for "power" in Acts 1:8 is *dunamis* in Greek. It means strength, power and ability. In this case, *dunamis* means the ability to touch the world, the power to work miracles and the strength to endure persecution. The word was adopted by Alfred E. Nobel to name the new explosive he invented—dynamite. For this reason, some preachers have characterized the baptism in the Holy

Spirit as God's dynamite. I am not comfortable with this characterization because the baptism doesn't blow us up but provides ability beyond our natural capability.

The baptism in the Holy Spirit had a dramatic effect on the life of Peter. A few days before Pentecost, a slave girl confronted Peter outside the hall where Jesus was on trial before the Sanhedrin. In response to her confrontation two different times, Peter denied he ever knew Jesus. When Peter was confronted a third time, he again denied knowing Jesus—and he did it with curses.

> While Peter was below in the courtyard, one of the servant girls of the high priest came by. When she saw Peter warming himself, she looked closely at him. "You also were with that Nazarene, Jesus," she said. But he denied it. "I don't know or understand what you're talking about," he said, and went out into the entryway. When the servant girl saw him there, she said again to those standing around, "This fellow is one of them." Again he denied it. After a little while, those standing near said to Peter, "Surely you are one of them, for you are a Galilean." He began to call down curses on himself, and he swore to them, "I don't know this man you're talking about."
>
> —MARK 14:66–71

Then, on the Day of Pentecost, *it was Peter* who stood up and spoke to the crowd assembled by the commotion. Acts 2:14–36 records:

> Then Peter stood up with the Eleven…"Therefore let all Israel be assured of this: God has made this Jesus, whom you crucified, both Lord and Christ."

Clearly, Peter is no longer the fearful disciple but the powerful apostle. Peter knew that his words would not be popular with those who chose to continue in their rejection of the Messiah. They crucified Jesus; Peter could have been next. But the Holy Spirit prompted the words Peter spoke, and they had their effect. The crowd was struck to the heart and repented wholesale.

Jesus intended His followers to function with much more than rhetorical boldness. He wanted the preaching of the Word to be followed with signs and wonders, God Himself verifying the preached Word. Jesus promised us the ability to perform such signs in John 14:12–17:

> I tell you the truth, anyone who has faith in me will do what I have been doing. He will do even greater things than these, because I am going to the Father. And I will do whatever you ask in my name, so that the Son may bring glory to the Father. You may ask me for anything in my name, and I will do it. If you love me, you will obey what I command. And I will ask the Father, and He will give you another Counselor to be with you forever—the Spirit of Truth. The world cannot accept him, because it neither sees him nor knows him. But you know him, for he lives with you and will be in you.

Jesus linked His promise of signs and wonders with the sending of the Holy Spirit. This is the baptism in the Holy Spirit that first took place at Pentecost. It was both for that time and for now. Peter promised the baptism to all whom God would call:

> Repent and be baptized, every one of you, in the

name of Jesus Christ for the forgiveness of your sins. And you will receive the gift of the Holy Spirit. The promise is for you and your children and for all who are far off—for all whom the Lord our God will call.

—ACTS 2:38–39

Some claim that what Peter was promising was salvation. Indeed, he was promising salvation, but he was promising more than that. Peter promised what they saw, the gift of the Holy Spirit as poured out on the Day of Pentecost.

Without this baptism we are unable to fulfill all that God wants for us—all He wants us to do and to be. Those present on the Day of Pentecost turned their world upside down (or rather right side up)! It could not have happened, as it cannot happen today, without the indwelling and empowerment of the Holy Spirit. The major keys to receiving the infilling of the Holy Spirit are loving Jesus and obeying Him. Those just seeking a new experience or the miraculous, without a heart of love and obedience toward Jesus, are just wasting their time.

For those who do love and obey Jesus, the baptism in the Holy Spirit is the gift Jesus promised us in Luke 11:13:

If you then, though you are evil, know how to give good gifts to your children, how much more will your Father in heaven give the Holy Spirit to those who ask him!

This gift is intended for those who are committed to being all God wants them to be. We all need every good gift that God, in His wisdom, planned for us. This world is too seductive and our enemy too shrewd for us to refuse any of God's gifts. We can trust Him.

WHAT TO EXPECT WHEN
ONE IS FILLED WITH THE SPIRIT

One of the first things those newly filled with the Holy Spirit discover is that a whole new world has opened up—the world of the Spirit. God originally formed man from the dust of the ground and breathed into his nostrils the breath of life, and man became a living being (or soul).[6] In Hebrew, the language of the Old Testament, the word translated "breath" also means "spirit" and "breeze." So man was composed of two things—earth and spirit—and the two uniting formed the soul. To the ancient Hebrews, the soul was understood as the totality of man's being. Most modern believers understand man to be a collection of three: body, soul and spirit. As God combined body with spirit, a new thing was created—soul. This is something like oxygen and hydrogen combining to form water, a new substance unlike the items that form it.

Both body and soul were affected as a result of man's sin, but his spirit is what died, having lost contact with God's Spirit. Salvation reunites our human spirit with God's Spirit, and we become whole again. The baptism in the Holy Spirit enables communication between our spirit and God's Spirit at a deeper level. The baptism allows our human spirit to communicate with God's Spirit at a level beyond that available through salvation alone.[7] It is this enhanced communication that is at the heart of all God does in and through the baptism in the Holy Spirit.

Suddenly, the Word of God is alive as never before. Verses seem to stand out on the page. Verses about encouragement, God's standards, passages relating to your calling—they seem to burn. This is the voice of God just as much as the whisper in your ear. This inner voice of God is also heightened as never before. With all this, the conviction of the Holy Spirit highlighting sin is also heightened. We must respond with repentance if we hope to achieve the destiny God has for us.

For some, the battle between God and Satan is instantly real, and they find themselves in the middle. Satan doesn't concern himself with most Christians. The reason is that most believers live their whole lives and make no impact on anyone for the kingdom. The enemy tries to keep people from salvation. He doesn't care how good or how religious someone is as long as his sins are not forgiven by Jesus. That person's destination is still hell, and Satan wins. Failing that, the enemy tries to keep believers ineffective in leading others to faith and spiritual maturity. Through the baptism in the Holy Spirit, we are empowered by God Himself to take Jesus' love and life to others.

The nine gifts of the Spirit, discussed in chapters 12 and 14 of 1 Corinthians, are all available to those who are filled with the Spirit. Through them, we partner with God—to act for God here on earth. Empowered by the Spirit, we can touch others with the power of God Himself. We can deliver God's hope and healing, His comfort and love.

Not only do we have access to the realm of the Spirit, but also He has more access to us. As a result, the fruit of the Spirit grow at an accelerated rate in our lives. We can more directly sense His love for us and His encouragement to love others. We feel His hurt when we fail to respond as He wants us to. All of this combines to help us grow more rapidly than we did before the baptism in the Holy Spirit.

Not only can we hear God's voice more clearly through the baptism in the Holy Spirit, but also we can sense the longings of God's heart. We can feel God's joy in worship or His sadness over those who are lost.

I can remember one occasion in my own life when I was present at a presentation of Jewish folk dances. Even though most of those who were dancing were not believers, I felt the heart of God leap for joy within me. The sensation really caught me by surprise. They were singing and dancing to music based on the Book of Psalms, music that worshiped God, and He was delighted.

The baptism in the Holy Spirit brings a new power in prayer. God can also give us prayer burdens. Through prayer, we give God permission to perform His will on earth. At times, God desires to act, but there is no one to grant Him permission. In these cases, He finds a Spirit-filled believer with whom He shares His desire. This often feels like a weight in the stomach. As the believer prays in the Spirit, the weight lifts. In Pentecostal circles this is called "praying through." Through the Holy Spirit we know God's desires and can partner with Him to pray them into existence. Through the Holy Spirit we can pray in accord with God's will in a way that would be impossible without His help:

> However, as it is written: "No eye has seen, no ear has heard, no mind has conceived what God has prepared for those who love him"—but God has revealed it to us by his Spirit. The Spirit searches all things, even the deep things of God. For who among men knows the thoughts of a man except the man's spirit within him? In the same way no one knows the thoughts of God except the Spirit of God.
>
> —1 CORINTHIANS 2:9–11

The Holy Spirit can even pray through us when we have no idea how to pray:

> In the same way, the Spirit helps us in our weakness. We do not know what we ought to pray for, but the Spirit himself intercedes for us with groans that words cannot express. And he who searches our hearts knows the mind of the Spirit, because the Spirit intercedes for the saints in accordance with God's will.
>
> —ROMANS 8:26–27

THE GIFT OF TONGUES AND THE BAPTISM

The gift of tongues has long been associated with the baptism in the Holy Spirit. Some denominations teach that tongues are the initial evidence of the baptism in the Holy Spirit. I would ask, "Evidence to whom?" Why is it important that the Christian community know whether or not an individual has been baptized in the Holy Spirit? Although it may be encouraging to see a fellow believer manifest this gift, the simple answer is that it isn't important for other Christians to know. We worship together, but our relationship with God comes down to a one-on-one matter.

My wife was raised in a church that taught that the gift of tongues was satanic. They argued that the gifts of the Spirit listed in the Book of 1 Corinthians ended as the New Testament canon of Scripture was finished. They claimed the gifts died with the apostle John. At the age of eighteen, she wanted more of God and asked Him for all that He had for her. She was baptized in the Holy Spirit at that time. She found a new world open to her (the world of the Spirit) without understanding what she perceived. The dominant

39

gift of the Spirit operating in her life at that time was discerning of spirits. It was years later when she learned about the baptism in the Holy Spirit and spoke in tongues. Yet, her early experience was very valid.

The question should not be, "Do I have to speak in tongues?" God intends the gift of tongues as a special prayer language for these latter days (since the Day of Pentecost). The Word says it builds up the individual.[8] If it is a gift from God, I want it! If it is to build me up, I need it!

There has also been some misunderstanding about the gift of tongues itself. It has two functions, as though it were two gifts in one. The first and primary use of the gift of tongues is in personal devotions. This is how the gift has been discussed to this point. The second use of the gift is in a public assembly. Here, it must be followed by an interpretation so that all may be blessed.[9] This misunderstanding about the duality of the gift caused churches to do what the apostle Paul said they should not do—deny the use of the gift altogether.[10]

TIMES AND SEASONS

Human beings are not built to live on an emotional "high." Following each high must come a low to allow the body to rest and prepare for the next high. Indeed, if we always lived on a high, it wouldn't seem like a high at all. We need the low points in our lives to appreciate the highs. In the same way, there are highs and lows in our spiritual lives.

Paul told Timothy that he should preach the gospel and "be prepared in season and out of season."[11] Paul indicated in this that there are times and seasons in ministry. There are times when the ministry of the Holy Spirit, with the gifts He brings, flows like a river. There are other times when nothing *seems* to happen. We need to trust our loving and faithful God that He is still there, still taking care of us and still concerned about our needs. We too need to learn to minister in and out of season.

In the same way, there are also times and seasons in God's dealings with churches. There are even times and seasons of the work of the Holy Spirit in the body of Christ as a whole. I initially called this work "Catch the Wave" because we are in the ground swells of a mighty End-Time *tsunami* of the Holy Spirit. "Catch the Wave" is helping many prepare to partner with God in this wave of His work.

A problem arises when we are not prepared for the ebb and flow of the Holy Spirit. Suddenly, we perceive our relationship with God and the Holy Spirit change. We assume we have done something to alienate God or that He is punishing us for something. Usually, nothing is farther from the truth. Of course, the enemy (Satan) takes the opportunity to throw in some slurs. Soon, we are convinced that we have committed the unpardonable sin when, all along, it is just a season.

Many believers worry at such times that they may have committed the unpardonable sin. Some denominations teach that there is no unpardonable sin, and that salvation is eternal and can never be lost. Contrary to this, the Word plainly states:

> It is impossible for those who have once been enlightened, who have tasted the heavenly gift, who have shared in the Holy Spirit, who have tasted the goodness of the word of God and the powers of the coming age, if they fall away, to be brought back to repentance, because to their loss they are crucifying the Son of God all over again and subjecting him to public disgrace.
> —HEBREWS 6:4–6

In 2 Timothy 3:16–17 Paul states, "All Scripture is God-breathed and is useful for teaching, rebuking, correcting and training in righteousness, so that the man of God may be thoroughly equipped for every good work." According to these verses, the Holy Spirit inspired the passage in Hebrews above. The Holy Spirit would not have placed these words in the Scriptures if the possibility of losing one's salvation did not exist. It is not something done easily, however.

Let's look at Hebrews 6:4–6 from the other point of view. Let's see what is involved in "falling away," or losing one's salvation. The passage starts with the statement "those who have once been enlightened." It seems that to lose one's salvation, a person must reject any enlightenment given by the Holy Spirit.

The next phrase in this passage says, "Who have tasted the heavenly gift, who have shared in the Holy Spirit." The heavenly gift is probably salvation itself. Through it we received not only forgiveness but also the gift of the Holy Spirit Himself. So to lose salvation, one must decide that he has been deluded and reject God's gift of the Holy Spirit and His power.

The next part of this passage says, "Who have tasted the goodness of the word of God." This would require thinking about the Bible as no more authoritative or valuable as a guide for life than any dime novel.

The author of Hebrews then writes, "Who have tasted... the powers of the coming age." This is a reference to the supernatural power of the Holy Spirit. This is the kind of power that turned water to wine, healed the lame and blind, and raised the dead. Tasting of that power would involve being used by God to deliver miracles. Losing salvation requires rejecting the miracle power of God—not just the power observed from afar, but also the power experienced firsthand.

Above all, to lose one's salvation, one must fall away from Jesus. It is the atoning death of Jesus on the cross and His resurrection that enable the forgiveness of sin. Without Jesus' atoning death and resurrection, God has no way to express His mercy. If a person falls that far, there is no longer any means of atonement. God's judgment is all that is left.

If a person has fallen that far, he no longer cares about the salvation Jesus offers. Indeed, it is that attitude of not caring that makes the unpardonable sin unpardonable. This is because he refuses to go to Jesus in repentance. Since there is no other forgiveness possible, he will experience God's judgment without mercy.

Deuteronomy 4:29 says, "If...you seek the LORD your God, you will find him if you look for him with all your heart and with all your soul." Those who consistently do that and are willing to repent are saved. They need not worry about committing the unpardonable sin because they care about being connected to God. Those who have fallen from salvation no longer worry about their relationship with God. The very fact that a person is concerned indicates that he has not committed the unpardonable sin. We need to trust God. When He said, "I will never leave you nor forsake you," He meant it.[12]

EMOTION AND THE BAPTISM

One young man I met long ago was in a home meeting where the baptism in the Holy Spirit was taught. As he saw others prayed for to receive the baptism, he saw them often burst into laughter. He saw this as a blasphemous response. We explained that those who burst into laughter were doing so in response to the overwhelming feeling of joy they experienced as the Holy Spirit filled them. After a few minutes of discussion, he asked us to pray for him to be filled with the Spirit. He added, "But I won't laugh!" We prayed. As the Holy Spirit fell on him, he started laughing and continued to laugh for a solid half-hour at least. When he finally stopped, he looked at us and said, "Now I understand."

Historically, some have claimed that the baptism in the Holy Spirit is, in fact, some group emotional experience of no authentic spiritual value. But baptism in the Holy Spirit is a personal encounter with God—an encounter that is typically more intense than any other human experience with the possible exception of initial salvation.

God is love.[13] He grieves,[14] and He longs for our fellowship.[15] He is an emotional God. When He created man, He made man with the same emotions He has. For this reason, it is understandable that encounters with God are often emotional experiences. My salvation was the first time I had cried in years. The night I was filled with the Holy Spirit was also an emotional night. But the essence of the experience is not emotion; it is an encounter with God. I have heard the testimony of a few people who received the baptism with no emotion at all. Almost all people are flooded with joy, peace, a feeling of being intensely loved or some other similar emotion.

How to Receive the Baptism

As you may have noticed, I do my best to keep this teaching practical. In this section, three simple steps will be given whereby any believer can be filled with the Holy Spirit. I encourage the reader to follow these steps and trust God to do the rest.

God only fills *believers* with the Holy Spirit. Catholic

Charismatics often lead those seeking the baptism through "the sinner's prayer" first. Commonly, people who grow up Catholic are never confronted with the requirement to accept Jesus as Savior. As a result, they think they are believers, and they are at some level, but they have not experienced salvation. If you are seeking the baptism, make sure you have a living relationship with Jesus first.[16]

1. Desire a deeper, more intense relationship with God.

When a group of people in Samaria were saved at the preaching of Philip, Peter and John went to them to be sure they got off on the right foot. Simon, a magician of some local fame, was among those saved. When Peter and John arrived, they prayed for each one to receive the baptism in the Holy Spirit. We don't know what was the outward expression of the Spirit's impact. It must have been something dynamic because Simon offered money to be able to impart the Holy Spirit. Simon wasn't interested in the effect the Spirit could have on his life or relationship with God; he just wanted a new trick. That was all he initially saw. Peter replied to Simon's offer, "May your money perish with you if you think that the gift of God is for sale."[17] In response to Peter's rebuke, Simon realized that he had made a major mistake and repented. Too often, believers see other believers speaking in tongues, bringing a word from the Lord through prophecy or telling tales of being led by the Spirit, and they want the same power. This desire, as strong as it may be, is not enough. As I have stated, the baptism is an encounter with God. It leads the believer into a deeper walk with God. It is this walk that God wants us to desire. This is *His* requirement for the baptism.

45

2. Simply ask God.

In Luke 11:9–13, Jesus talks about good fathers not giving their children a snake rather than a fish, or a scorpion rather than an egg. Then Jesus says, "If you then, though you are evil, know how to give good gifts to your children, how much more will your Father in heaven give the Holy Spirit to those who ask Him!" The Father's desire for all believers is that they be filled with the Holy Spirit. But they must ask. He will never force His will on any of us. As soon as we are ready to receive and ask, with the right motives, He will fill us to the extent we allow Him.

3. Accept it by faith.

Let God do the work. Something may happen immediately. If it does, great! Sometimes, even when we ask, we may not allow the Holy Spirit to take control. The baptism is a step in a progressive transformation of our lives—from *our* lordship to *God's* lordship. For this reason, occasionally, believers have to go though a growing experience before they can be filled with the Holy Spirit in a tangible way. God is still faithful. If nothing seems to happen, keep seeking God and His purposes for your life. By doing this, you enable Him to remove whatever hinders you from receiving all that God has for you.

There are many believers who would never consider themselves Pentecostal or Charismatic, yet they have been filled with the Holy Spirit. Why? Because they have sincerely asked for all God had for them. But their theology did not allow for tongues or other charismatic gifts, so those gifts didn't happen. What they got from the baptism was a closer walk with God and greater inspiration. God gave them all they were willing to accept.

Chapter Four

The Gifts
of the Spirit

There are a number of lists of gifts Jesus gives to His church. Most are lists of ministries or offices in the church. The list of gifts in 1 Corinthians 12 is different. These are empowerments for ministry. My pastor, Dr. James Reeve, calls them "God's power tools for ministry." These gifts allow a believer to minister in a realm beyond himself and his own abilities.

In 1 Corinthians 12:4, the word translated "gifts" is *charisma* in the Greek. The Greek root word *charis* is translated "grace." So, literally, these are grace-gifts. Gifts are given freely to believers, as the Holy Spirit distributes them. Each gift is an act of grace; each shows God's favor to His people.

WHO GETS THE GIFTS

One of the first matters that must be firmly established is who gets the gifts. First Corinthians 12:4–7 says:

There are different kinds of gifts, but the same
Spirit. There are different kinds of service, but the
same Lord. There are different kinds of working,
but the same God works all of them in all men.
Now to each one the manifestation of the Spirit is
given for the common good.

Look at that last sentence (v. 7). To the person who minis-
ters the gift, it is a "manifestation of the Spirit." It manifests
or makes visible the invisible Holy Spirit within. It is a gift
to those who receive it—just as a man dressed in a brown
uniform, driving a brown truck, shows up on your doorstep
with a brown box. The box is not a gift for the man in
brown; he's just delivering it. The gift is for you. In the same
way, the one ministering the gift is just manifesting the Holy
Spirit within. The gift is from God to the individual or
group who will receive it.

This seems like a minor distinction, but it is not. Some
have been taught that a believer receives only one gift. In
fact, as I read the New Testament, the gifts seem resident in
the Holy Spirit Himself. Any Spirit-filled believer can manifest *any* of the gifts according to three requirements:

1. Need—God does nothing just for show.

2. God's desire to meet the need—there is no
    way to force Him to work.

3. The believer's willingness to deliver the gift.

In practice, an individual may flow predominantly in one
gift. This is only due to the individual's personality and experience. As the individual continues to grow in his abilities in
the Spirit, he will become proficient in other gifts as well.

The gifts of the Spirit in 1 Corinthians 12 will be discussed as they fall into three arbitrary categories: gifts of speaking, gifts of knowing and gifts of doing. Each category contains three gifts of similar function.

GIFTS OF SPEAKING

The gifts of speaking, for the purposes of our discussion, include the gifts of tongues, prophecy and interpretation of tongues. Each of these gifts is exercised through speaking.

Tongues

The first in this group is "tongues," or languages. One reason for confusion in some churches over this gift is that it has two expressions. The first and most important is for private devotions. It edifies the believer[1] and can be used to communicate with God at a level that can never be known in one's native language.[2] Paul wrote, "For anyone who speaks in a tongue does not speak to men but to God. Indeed, no one understands him; he utters mysteries with his spirit."[3] If God created it for my edification, I want it!

The second expression of tongues mentioned in the Word is in a group setting. Paul wrote, "What then shall we say, brothers? When you come together, everyone has a hymn, or a word of instruction, a revelation, a tongue or an interpretation. All of these must be done for the strengthening of the church. If anyone speaks in a tongue, two—or at the most three—should speak, one at a time, and someone must interpret. If there is no interpreter, the speaker should keep quiet in the church and speak to himself and God."[4] Here, the importance is that the group is edified as a whole, rather than individual believers speaking in tongues and edifying themselves at the expense of the group. For this reason, when a tongue is delivered in a congregational setting, the leader of the service should pause and wait for the interpretation.

These are "the tongues of men and of angels."[5] That is, some of these languages are known among mankind, and some of the languages are not known. In all cases, the language bypasses the brain and comes from the human spirit, enabled by the Holy Spirit. Paul said, "If I pray in a tongue, my spirit prays, but my mind is unfruitful. So what shall I do? I will pray with my spirit, but I will also pray with my mind; I will sing with my spirit, but I will also sing with my mind."[6] One can sing in the Spirit (singing in tongues) to a standard tune or to a tune made up in the moment.

Because the mind is bypassed when one speaks in a tongue, some have postulated that the act of speaking or praying in tongues requires some mystical or hypnotic trance. This is not true. A Spirit-filled believer can turn the tongues on and off at will, and it requires only an act of the will. For this reason, a number of Spirit-filled believers have a problem "learning" to speak in tongues. They have difficulty allowing the sounds to bypass the mind.

I was teaching this one day when I suddenly realized how to help people who know they are filled with the Spirit but have never spoken in tongues. I encourage them to go alone into a room of their house or in their car. Then pray something like, "Father, I know that I am filled with the Holy Spirit. I ask you to help me manifest the gift of tongues. For the next few minutes I will praise you with whatever sounds come into my head." And start doing just that. I tell them not to say words, but just worship with sounds. At the worst, the person will bless God's socks off! Here is His kid, trying to grow in the ability to manifest the Spirit by worshiping Him. How could God not be blessed! Eventually, as one repeats this process, the sounds will form themselves into a language, a tongue. Be patient. Babies are not born saying, "Good morning, Mother; I would like a drink of milk now." They must learn to speak properly over a period of time. The same is true of tongues.

Finally, note that Paul considered tongues to be such a vital part of his life that he told the Corinthian believers, "I thank God that I speak in tongues more than all of you."[7] If it was that important to Paul, the author of most of the New Testament, then we need to regard it with similar importance.

Prophecy

When most people think of prophecy, they think of foretelling the future. Biblical prophecy, however, is forth-telling the mind and intentions of God. Often, rather than delivering a certainty from God, the prophecy is contingent upon man's response. In fact, prophecy is frequently used by God to elicit man's response. Paul wrote, "But everyone who prophesies speaks to men for their strengthening, encouragement and comfort."[8] This is the purpose of the gift.

Prophecy is usually delivered in the first person, as though God Himself is speaking. The person prophesying may add, "Thus says the Lord…" or "God is saying…" Through prophecy, God draws focus to things He wants to do among His people. It will never contradict the written Word, which is God's primary revelation to man.

Some believers are against prophecy because they view it as adding to the written Word of God, the Bible. On the contrary, prophecy often draws our focus to specific areas of the Word. Even when it doesn't, words of prophecy are never to be regarded as on the same level as the Bible. Note that there were many prophets in the Old Testament whose words were never included in the Bible. This was not because their gift was not from God, but rather because their prophetic words were of a different nature and scope.

There are two Greek words translated into English as "word." The first is *logos*, meaning "a written word." It also means the logical structure that goes into a written communication of thought. In fact, the word *logic* comes from *logos*. The second Greek word is *rhema*, meaning "the sound of the voice." *Rhema* words are more temporal in scope. Prophetic words are of this type.

For this reason, as a general opinion of the author, one should not write down or otherwise record a prophecy given to him or her. The prophecy is given to a person in a particular situation at a particular time. If recorded and later replayed, the differences in the setting at the time of replay could alter the perceived meaning of the prophecy. One exception to this is when the prophetic word relates to one's destiny. I encourage people to do everything possible to never forget words of destiny.

God's primary way of communicating with individual believers is one on one, directly from His Spirit to our spirit. Prophecy must, then, confirm what the person feels God is directly saying to him or her. If not, don't reject the prophecy, but pray about the prophetic word and listen to God. If it remains unconfirmed by God's direct communications, reject it as being from an overly zealous believer.

The discussion thus far has centered on hearing God's voice. God can communicate in many more ways than verbally. He can use pictures, impressions and dreams, to list a few. He can also use combinations of these. When God gives me a prophecy, I usually get a picture with the words. This seems to be intended to fully communicate God's desires to me so that I can more clearly communicate them as I deliver the prophecy. God communicates His message using the personality and basic nature of the person prophesying. Two people may prophesy the same basic message but in totally different ways based upon their different levels of education, knowledge of the Word and general life experience.

I have been prophesying for long enough that I can tell God's voice from my own or the voice of the enemy. It was not always so. When I first started prophesying, I was not sure if what I was hearing was from God or myself. I then would ask God to make me sure. As a result of my inquiry, God would pour power down on me. My teeth would tingle. Do you know how hard it is to make teeth tingle?

It's God's responsibility to communicate to us in a way so that we know it is God. Once He communicates to us, it becomes our responsibility to obey and deliver what He has delivered to us. So if you think God is giving you instructions or a prophecy, but are not sure, ask Him. Be sure to obey once you know for sure. A later section will deal with hearing God's voice in more detail.

There is one other thing I want to mention about my early days of delivering prophecy. God usually gave me a partial sentence. As I was obedient to deliver the part I was given, He then gave me more. I had to be willing to make a fool of myself should God leave me hanging. I had to trust Him to come through for me. He always did! Now, He usually gives me full sentences but usually not a full prophetic message.

It is easy to want to editorialize on what the Holy Spirit is saying through you, especially when the Spirit gives you a partial sentence. This temptation must be resisted at all cost. Otherwise the person prophesying is placing his words in

God's mouth. I have run into this many times, but God did something special on one occasion. A person was prophesying in a meeting I attended, and God gave me, word for word, what He gave the other person. The Spirit gave him words he was repeating. Then suddenly, he started adding his own words. The Holy Spirit waited patiently for the person to finish. Then the Holy Spirit resumed His message. This happened three or four times in his prophecy. After the meeting, I took him aside and discussed the matter with him. God let me see what was going on that one time so I could correct that person and help him to grow in that area.

The best of us is still human and can make mistakes in hearing God's voice. For this reason, Paul told the Corinthians, "Two or three prophets should speak, and the others should weigh carefully what is said."[9] By implication, those who were to judge were other prophets. We can all judge a word of prophecy as to whether or not it lines up with the Bible—and it must! A prophet, however, judges prophecy by checking the heart of God. True words ring true. Whether the word rings true or not, the goal is to encourage each other to grow.

Interpretation of tongues

The third gift of speaking is the gift of interpreting tongues. This gift works much the same as prophecy and follows a message in tongues delivered in a group meeting.

Because of its similarity to prophecy, we will say little about this gift. One thing we do need to say is that this is interpretation, not translation. The message in tongues may be long and the interpretation may be short, but both may be valid.

Because one is speaking to God when speaking in

tongues, some have argued that a message in tongues in church must sound like a psalm when interpreted. Since the interpretation usually sounds more like prophecy, they say that what has taken place is a tongue followed by prophecy rather than interpretation. This may sometimes be the case. But in any case, the Spirit is speaking to His church. How He chooses to do this is His business.

One of the less common examples of interpretation of tongues occurred to my oldest son, James. He went to Bishkek, Kurgistan on a mission team. He was in a prayer meeting. A group of believers were all standing around in a circle. Some were Russians, and some were members of the mission team. Some were praying and some prophesying, each in turn. A member of the Russian church stood and began to prophesy. As he spoke, James heard Russian but understood in English!

GIFTS OF KNOWING

This is a group of gifts that deal primarily with the mind. They enable precise ministry. Occasionally, God wishes to deal with an area, but the person receiving ministry is reluctant to reveal himself. God can use these gifts to direct the person ministering to probe the area, often resulting in tears and deliverance.

Word of knowledge

The first gift of knowing we will deal with, one of the most powerful gifts, is the gift of knowledge. God tells the person ministering things that the person could have no way of knowing otherwise. The story of the woman at the well is a good example.

To understand the story one needs a quick history and

geography lesson. When Joshua led the people into the Promised Land, the land was only divided by tribal lines. Years later when Solomon died, Rehoboam became king over Judea to the south. Jeroboam, one of Solomon's officers, rebelled and became king over Israel to the north.[10] Omri, a later king of Israel, built a city to serve as his capital, naming it Samaria.[11] He set up a polluted form of Jewish worship in the city to prevent the people from returning to Jerusalem to worship at the temple. Those living in the far north of Israel didn't go along with the false religion and remained true to God. Samaria was conquered by the Assyrians as God's judgment on their sin.[12] The Assyrians shipped in people from other areas and cultures and shipped out many of the Israelites. The Israelites left in the area intermarried with the new people, violating a restriction against marrying outside the faith. By Jesus' time, the city had been destroyed, and the name "Samaria" had been applied to a region between Judea in the south and the area around the Sea of Galilee in the north.

This passage begins with Jesus saying that He must go through Samaria.[13] For most good Jews, this was not true. The preferred route to Galilee from Judea was to cross the Jordan River, walk up the flat Jordan River valley and cross again into Galilee. They would do this for two reasons. First of all, the walking was easier than walking through the mountainous region of Samaria.

The second reason was religious. People of the area were despised by the full-blooded Jews of Judea and Galilee because of their odd worship and because they had intermarried with foreigners. The believing Jews would have nothing to do with those in the area of Samaria. This was especially true for rabbis. But Jesus had an appointment in

Samaria. That was why He had to go through that region.

When Jesus got to Sychar His appointment was waiting for Him, without even knowing it. Jesus asked her for a drink, and she instantly sensed the oddity of His request. In addition to being a despised Samaritan, she was also a woman. Rabbis did not speak to women to whom they were not married. As a third strike against her, she was an outcast in her own town. We can tell this because had she been acceptable company to the other ladies of the town, she would have drawn water in the cool of the morning rather than at noon. She asked Jesus why He was speaking to her.[14]

In Jesus' answer He spoke of living water. Most (if not

all) commentators go off on that, without even noting that Jesus answered her question. Jesus said, "If you knew the gift of God and who it is that asks you for a drink, you would have asked him…"[15] Jesus said that she would have asked Him if she had realized who He was. Jesus was there because, through the word of knowledge, He knew that she had an open heart. Imagine how powerful for an evangelist to be directed to ripe fruit, as Jesus was, rather than trying to pick green fruit.

Jesus gives us a more obvious example of word of knowledge later in the discussion to bring her to a point of personal confrontation. Jesus reveals that she had five husbands and was currently living in sin with a sixth man.[16] These are all things Jesus could not naturally know if God the Father had not told Him through the Holy Spirit.

When someone is ministering with a strong word of knowledge, there can often be a fear in the congregation that the person ministering knows all about each of them. This fear is not founded in truth. The Holy Spirit will give specific words about specific points of ministry, but the Holy Spirit is a gentleman; He will not violate one's privacy.

Word of wisdom

The word of knowledge provides information that could not otherwise be known. In the same way, a word of wisdom tells us *how* to minister. Jesus lived and ministered with the word of wisdom in operation, but examples of it are much harder to find than examples of word of knowledge. Even so, I believe one example is in John 7:1–7.

The passage opens by saying that Jesus was avoiding Judea because the Jewish leaders were out for His head. But the Feast of Tabernacles was coming, and Jesus was under a religious obligation to go. For Him to be our Savior, He had to show up. Jesus' family taunted Him by encouraging Him to show the miracles He did in upper-class Judea rather than just in backwoods Galilee. They didn't believe in Him at the time.

Jesus replied, "You go to the Feast. I am not yet going up to this Feast, because for me the right time has not yet come."[17] As soon as they left for the feast, Jesus also left for the feast. It seems that Jesus could have just gone with His family, but Jesus didn't follow the world's expectations, religious conventions or public desires. He moved at God's direction and on His timetable. Often, the rhythm of God is just a bit out of sync with the rhythm of the world. But following God's beat makes all the difference.

Calling the gift "word of wisdom" implies that each word is an individual chunk of wisdom, given for a specific time and situation. Each chunk of wisdom stands on its own— individual gifts of wisdom from God. These are gifts of His perspective for ministry.

Discerning of spirits

The gift of discerning of spirits is a gift of insight into another realm: the realm of the Holy Spirit and the angels as well as the realm of demon spirits. The purpose of the gift is to allow us to battle the enemy and help others minister at the Holy Spirit's direction.

I recall being in one meeting where, for some reason, God chose me to be the leader. During the meeting, I detected the Holy Spirit anointing one person for a prophetic word. As I closed my eyes, I saw the Holy Spirit move in my mind's eye. I could then open my eyes and see with whom He was dealing. After dealing with one person for a while, He moved to the next person, and then the next, until someone finally gave the prophecy. I was then able to describe what happened to the group. This verified that it really was the Holy Spirit who was impressing them with a word.

The main use of the gift is to detect the work of the enemy and to direct powerful ministry. This gift allows believers to determine if someone's odd behavior is due to the presence of a demon or some more natural reason, like mental illness. Through the gift we can determine when we are having a bad hair day or are under a real demonic attack.

On the subject of demon possession, there is a great deal of misunderstanding in the body of Christ, the church. The word *possession* implies ownership. There is no way any demon can own a human being. The word translated "demon possessed" in the New Testament is *daimonizomai* in Greek. It combines the word for an evil spirit (*daimon*) with a word meaning to suffer loss through violence (*zemia*). It basically means simply to have or hold a demon. "Demonized" (harassed by a demon) may be a better rendering than "demon possessed."

Some claim that believers can not be demonized because they are indwelt by the Holy Spirit. In my experience and in the experience of others, a believer is indwelt by whatever being to which he yields himself. Yielding to God, he is "possessed" by the Holy Spirit. By resisting God and yielding to the enemy's persuasion, he is open to being "possessed" by an evil spirit. There is no gift of casting out demons. Power over demons is based on the authority purchased by Jesus on the cross and is given to every believer. Our ability to draw on that authority is based on our individual commitment to the lordship of Jesus in our everyday lives. This will be discussed in detail in the next chapter.

Gifts of Doing

The third category of gifts is gifts of doing. These are gifts where God steps out of His realm and into ours, suspending the laws of physics to work His will. Again, He has chosen to require our involvement. If we choose not to act at His prompting, He won't act.

Gifts of healing

"Gifts of healing" is always plural. There is no gift to heal. As with other gifts, the person delivering the gift is simply the means God uses. Each healing is a separate gift of God's grace to the one who needs healing.

As a gift of God's grace, it cannot be demanded or cajoled into existence if God, in His wisdom, chooses not to act. Our faith cannot compel God to act either. As I have said before, God has no crank on His side that says, "Turn here for a miracle." If He chooses to act, in partnership with our faith, He will. Our part is simply to trust Him and be available to deliver whatever He chooses to send.

Consider the lame man at the "beautiful gate" of the temple in Acts 3:1–8. Peter and John were just entering the temple as they had hundreds of times before. To do so, they had to pass this lame man who regularly sat begging at the gate. This day was different. As Peter and John passed the man this day, the Holy Spirit prompted the apostles to act. The lame man was asking everyone who passed for money. Peter said to him, "Look at us!" drawing his attention to them. The lame man assumed that they were going to give him money. He had no idea what he was about to receive.

Peter, prompted by the Holy Spirit, said, "Silver or gold I do not have, but what I have I give you. In the name of Jesus Christ of Nazareth, walk." Peter grabbed the man's arms and lifted him to his feet, a really dangerous thing to do if he was not positive that God would heal him. As he pulled him to his feet, God healed his legs. The man entered the temple for the first time in his life, and his joy was obvious.

Jesus must have passed the man many times as he begged for coins. Jesus never healed him. It was not God's time for the man. Then, Jesus was put to death. If the man was waiting for Jesus to heal him, Jesus' death must have crushed his hopes. When he least expected healing, along came Peter and John. Why did it take so long? Why didn't Jesus just reach down and touch him, imparting healing? What was so special about that day? These are questions no one can answer—not for this lame man and not for those who need healing today. God is sovereign.

I often find that our perspective on healing is skewed away from reality. If our bodies are healed in this life, the healing is temporary. God is just postponing the entry into eternity. As believers, we must acknowledge that most of our lives will be lived with God, beyond this life. As such, this life becomes just a boot camp for eternity. Earthly healing is nice, but being taken home to God is a permanent healing. Psalm 116:15 says, "Precious in the sight of the LORD is the death of his saints."

Does God, then, not want to heal us? God loves us and endured being whipped to provide healing for us.[18] Healing our bodies is a priority to the Lord, but it is not His highest priority. If we can grow as God wants us to with healing, He will heal us. If, in His wisdom, He knows that healing our bodies will stand in the way of growing our spirit, we must forego the physical healing, at least for the moment.

When a gift of healing occurs, it may be instantaneous or it may happen gradually. If it does take place instantaneously, it falls under the category of working of miracles as well. Healing must not be thought of as limited to instantaneous events. Many miraculous healings take place over days or even years. They are, nevertheless, divine healings.

As an example, the woman who became my wife was attending Cal State University at Los Angeles in the 1960s. One morning, on her drive to school, the traffic in front of her stopped. She stopped her station wagon. The woman behind her didn't even slow down. She hit my wife's car going over sixty miles an hour. The paramedics who came to extricate my wife from the twisted remains of her car said that if she had not been driving a station wagon, she would not have lived. She spent the next year in bed with severe neck and back injures. She slowly recovered, but the doctors told her that she would never turn her head normally again. Even years after we were married, she would experience extended periods of pain caused by muscle cramps. She could not sit in one position for more than an hour. Her healing took a total of about ten years, but now she is totally healed.

There are so many reported healings in Jesus' ministry that it is hard to draw a single example to place here. Note, however, that each recorded healing was performed in a unique way. In each case, Jesus was following the instructions of His Father delivered though the Holy Spirit. For this reason, we need to avoid falling into a set pattern when delivering gifts of healing.

Working of miracles

The gifts of working of miracles are literally "works of power" in the original Greek. Here, God suspends the laws of physics, which were created as part of the physical universe, for a brief moment. For instance, God suspended physical laws to turn water into wine.

God's miracles are done in such a way that they defy analysis. He usually performs miracles when people are not watching. Things just seem to change from one moment to the next. Jesus' first miracle of turning water to wine is a good example.[19] Did the water change when the water pots were filled? Perhaps when the first ladle was drawn out? Or was it some time in between? Even those who performed the actions could not answer the questions.

Here too God does nothing without our participation. That is the reason for this gift of the Holy Spirit. He has committed earth into our keeping.[20] No matter how much God wants to intervene on earth, He will not do so without being invited by a human being. As we respond to His prompting and act in faith, we enable God to act.

Faith

I usually don't like to use the term *faith* because the word implies different things to different believers. True faith is simply trust—trust in God. Some believers seem to think of faith as a way to manipulate God, as though they could force God to act by believing in some desired outcome from prayer. Jesus always taught that faith was to be placed in God, not in a desired outcome.

For example, in Mark 11, Jesus curses a fig tree. The next day, His disciples were astonished that the tree withered so quickly. Jesus sensed a teachable moment and gave us the well-known teaching about mountain-moving faith. He began by saying, "Have faith in God."[21] God is always the focus of our faith. We trust Him to perform His will.

There are three kinds of faith: saving faith, growing faith

and the gift of faith. The first kind, saving faith, is given by the Holy Spirit.[22] Through saving faith, we enter into a relationship with God. Most true Christians can point to some time in the past when suddenly they just knew that the gospel was true—that Jesus is God, lived a sinless life, died for their sins, arose from the dead, and that God was offering forgiveness. This assurance of the truth of the Gospel is saving faith.

The second kind of faith naturally grows as we experience life as a believer. As we trust God, and He is found faithful, we learn to trust Him more. Our faith grows from encounter to encounter. In the first chapter I shared a story of being laid-off. During that period, God provided for my financial needs. When I started work again and received my first paycheck, I still had a few dollars in the bank. Years later, after getting married and having two children, I was out of work again. I was able to trust God for my needs during that time because I had been through a similar experience in which God was found trustworthy. My faith had grown because of the former experience.

The third kind of faith is the gift of faith. It usually accompanies the gifts of healings and miracles. Through the gift of faith we can trust God for the truly impossible. The gift of faith allows God to do miracles. When the gift of faith is active, we are absolutely positive that God will do exactly what we have asked Him to do. It seems at that moment that nothing is impossible...and then the gift goes away until needed the next time. Our level of faith, or trust in God, returns to normal.

A FINAL WORD ABOUT GIFTS

The important part about ministering the gifts of the Holy

Spirit is not an ability to properly classify them, but rather just to allow God to perform His will. There are many miracles He wants to work: healings to deliver, people to set free from the devil and lives set free from their own past. All He requires is someone to partner with Him. Any believer *can* partner with God's miraculous work. All one needs is to listen to God's voice and obey. He will do the rest. No one responds perfectly to the prompting of the Holy Spirit. Don't give up if you make a mistake. Learn from your mistakes and try again!

Chapter Five

Spiritual Warfare

The more we learn about the universe, the more we discover that God created the entire universe to have a place
where mankind could live. This is also the place were Satan
was imprisoned long before man was created. Ezekiel
28:14–17 talks about Lucifer as being created to be the
guardian cherub for God's throne. When he sinned through
pride, God exiled him to this planet and he became Satan.
His name literally means *adversary* in Hebrew.

THE "WORLD" IS CONTROLLED BY DEMONS

When Satan fell, one-third of all the angels fell with him. In
Revelation 12, the earthly life, death and resurrection of
Jesus are placed in metaphorical language. Satan is por-
trayed as an enormous red dragon with seven heads and ten
horns. His tail swept one-third of the stars out of the sky.[1]
Most commentators agree that these stars are angels that
followed Satan in sin and became demons.

Even before God placed Adam and Eve on earth, God
knew that Eve would be deceived and Adam would choose

67

to follow his wife into sin rather than remain obedient to God. God knew that Jesus would have to become human to redeem mankind.[2] God still chose to place us here, knowing that there would be some who would choose Him. It is apparently for the joy of receiving these few that God did it. It is said of Jesus in Hebrews 12:2:

> Let us fix our eyes on Jesus, the author and per-fecter of our faith, who for the joy set before him endured the cross, scorning its shame, and sat down at the right hand of the throne of God.

Apparently in Old Testament times, angels were given the responsibility of keeping Satan and his demons in check. We get a glimpse of this in the Book of Daniel. At one point Daniel prayed and partially fasted for three weeks. At the end of this time, Daniel was met by an angel. The angel said that he had been delayed for the entire period of Daniel's fast by "the prince of the Persian kingdom," a powerful demon who exerted influence over that pagan empire. The angel said that he was finally able to proceed because "Michael, one of the chief princes, came to help me." Jude 9 refers to Michael as an archangel. The angel who appeared to Daniel also said that he was returning to fight against "the prince of Persia."[3]

DELIVERANCE COMES THROUGH THE CROSS

Jesus won the major victory over Satan and sealed his fate on the cross:

> And having disarmed the [satanic] powers and authorities, he made a public spectacle of them, triumphing over them by the cross.
>
> —COLOSSIANS 2:15

The Roman legions would lead stripped captives in

chains through the streets of Rome to celebrate their victory over other lands. Here, Paul uses the same language to speak of Jesus' victory over Satan.

In this age, as a result of Jesus' victory, Satan and his minions wield a fraction of the power he had in the Old Testament. Satan has been left here to be our adversary. Paul tells the Ephesians that "our struggle is not against flesh and blood, but against the rulers, against the authorities, against the powers of this dark world and against the spiritual forces of evil in the heavenly realms."[4] It may appear that evangelists and missionaries are trying to convert people from superstitious practices and fatalistic religion. In reality, their beliefs and practices are "doctrines of devils."[5] Satan tempts us to sin and then tells us we are unworthy of God's love, as if any human righteousness could be adequate. That is why Jesus died for us, to make us worthy! Even when believers battle depression and low self-esteem, they are fighting the influence of the enemy.

By standing against him, we are strengthened. This is like a tribal boy learning to hunt by killing a goat tied to a stake.

Authority Comes Through Relationship

There is no gift of casting out demons. That is an authority given to every believer based on one's individual relationship to Jesus. Jesus has already won the victory over the enemy. The more we line up with God's authority by our obedience, the more we take part in Jesus' victory. This can be demonstrated in two passages. The first is a tale of the seven sons of a Jewish chief priest named Sceva. They were Jewish exorcists. They saw Paul cast out demons in the name of Jesus. It seemed much easier than the means they usually employed. They got a demon-possessed man cornered in a house and tried to cast the demon out in the name of Jesus whom Paul preached. To this, the demon spoke through the possessed man and said, "Paul I know and Jesus I know, but who are you?" The man sent all seven sons of Sceva from the house naked and bleeding.[6] They had tried to use Jesus' power and authority with no relationship to draw upon.

A second passage that demonstrates the power of relationship in wielding Jesus' authority is the story of the Roman centurion. He came to Jesus to seek healing for his servant who was sick. Jesus was ready to go with the centurion to his house when the centurion stopped him. He said, "Lord, I do not deserve to have you come under my roof. But just say the word, and my servant will be healed. For I myself am a man under authority, with soldiers under me. I tell this one, 'Go,' and he goes; and that one, 'Come,' and he comes. I say to my servant, 'Do this,' and he does it."[7] The centurion recognized that Jesus had divine power because He was in line with God's authority. The centurion was able to see this because of his own relationship to the authority of Rome.

But just being a believer is not enough in many cases. Jesus was in a sinless relationship with His Father—a relationship so intimate that Jesus said, "Anyone who has seen me has seen the Father."[8] Jesus had God's full authority over the enemy. His disciples occasionally had trouble. When Jesus was on the "mount of transfiguration," His disciples were dealing with a demon-possessed boy with no success. When Jesus came down from the mountain, He dealt with the demon, setting the boy free. Jesus' disciples asked Him why they were unable to dislodge the demon. In reply, Jesus said, "This kind can come out only by prayer and fasting."[9] The purpose of prayer and fasting is to improve our relationship with God, thus increasing our authority.

It is not our righteousness that gives us authority. The best of our righteousness is as filthy rags.[10] We have righteousness the same way we have authority over the enemy—through Jesus' cross. For this reason, speaking lightly about the elements of our salvation can undercut our authority. My pastor, Dr. James Reeve, shared one occasion when he attempted to deal with a demon. He said he was not successful because he had been joking about the cross, the blood of Jesus and the name of Jesus. That occasion taught him never to make light of the elements of our power and of Jesus' redemption.

SATAN'S PLAN AND JESUS' BLOOD

Hollywood portrays Satan as an incredibly powerful being, something like the dragon that rose through the church altar in the movie *End of Days*. Hollywood makes him seem like a being so strong that it takes an Arnold Schwarzenegger and a lot of luck to defeat him. The truth is that Satan has already been defeated at the cross. The only power he can wield is the power we give him.

Today, Satan wields power in two areas:

1. He has power where he is allowed to work, being given authority by humans.

2. He usurps power over nonbelievers and over believers who do not use the authority Jesus purchased on the cross.

Pagans view Satan's power as a neutral force that humans can manipulate using talismans and spells. These include white witches and warlocks as well as mystics who practice other religions. They think that they can use this force for whatever they desire. White witches and warlocks try to use the force for good, to serve a god. But Satan doesn't take orders from humans easily. He extracts a penalty for the power they manipulate. The end result is that those who use Satan's power end up as his captives. Black witches and warlocks are different only in that they realize that it is satanic power they manipulate.

Even some believers use the elements of redemption as talismans. For instance, some believers "plead the blood of Jesus" over all sorts of objects as a shield against Satan. They argue that it worked so well at the first Passover. The ancient Hebrews placed the blood of a spotless lamb on the lintel and doorposts of their houses to protect them from the angel of death.[11] The only problem with this argument is that the angel of death was God's angel. The blood protected them from the wrath of God, not Satan. This is the same way the blood of Jesus protects us from the wrath of God today.

The Word tells us that the blood of Jesus was shed for the forgiveness of our sins. At the Last Supper, Jesus took the cup and said, "This is my blood of the covenant, which is poured out for many *for the forgiveness of sins.*"[12] His blood redeems us from sin and the power of darkness, sanctifies us, cleanses our conscience and gives us direct and immediate access to our heavenly Father.[13]

Hidden sin can provide a point of attachment like the handle on a pitcher from which Satan can assert influence in the lives of believers. This doesn't mean that a person so affected is demon possessed. It means that he has made a place for a demon to be a part of his or her life.[14] No matter how the person tries, he is unable to rid himself of the evil influence until the hidden sin is dealt with, confessed and forgiven. Even when the sin is recurring, if he confesses the sin and repents at each occurrence, God forgives and accepts him.[15] Confession and repentance allow God to forgive him and completely remove the sin from him. This is the true work of the blood of Jesus in our lives. The blood cleanses away those handles, and Satan has nothing to latch onto.[16]

The Old Testament Hebrew word *shuwb*, translated "repent," literally means "to turn or turn back." Repenting based on this word means to turn to God and turn away from sin. One of the recurring problems in the church is caused when people only "pent"; they only turn to God without turning from sin, or they turn from sin without fully turning to God and accepting His lordship.

The New Testament Greek word *metanoeo*, translated "repent," means "to change the mind." This is not meant as just an intellectual exercise but a change of mind that results in a change of behavior. God doesn't demand that we clean up our act by our own strength. Rather, He demands a desire and decision to change. God will take that small offering and, over time, produce a lasting change in us. The process of change often demands that we continue to repent as we continue to fall into sin. The problem is not that we decide to sin knowing that we can repent and be forgiven. Rather, our inner sin nature holds us captive to sin until, through repeated repentance and forgiveness, God heals that part of our fallen nature. God's grace maintains our relationship with Him as this process continues. And it will continue while we are still in this body.

Most people think that Satan's goal is to make good people bad and bad people worse. In reality, his goal is just to keep people from Jesus. He wants to keep as many people as possible from heaven and take them with him to hell. Those who do not acknowledge Jesus as Savior are already under God's wrath.[17] They will end up in hell unless they eventually repent. Satan is pleased if he can lie, trick or scare people out of trusting Jesus as Savior.[18]

Believers who waver in their commitment to the lordship of Jesus or who are ignorant of the Word of God are susceptible to the enemy's lies. Satan makes sin fun and makes people think of God as the ultimate killjoy and tyrant. Once a believer gives in to sin, Satan then tells him that he has committed the unpardonable sin and is no longer acceptable to God no matter how sincerely he repents. This is, of course, a lie.

Those set on worshiping God are led astray into any one of a hundred false religions. Satan doesn't care which one is chosen as long as it doesn't acknowledge Jesus as Savior. The best way to hide a diamond is among a handful of zircons. Satan can't disguise the gospel, but he can confuse things by producing as many fakes as possible.

My wife and I went to Japan for our twenty-fifth anniversary. I had been sent there on about six trips by my work. This was my chance to play tour guide. We visited many Buddhist temples. Most of them had no satanic power in them. The Japanese who worship there do so primarily out of duty and tradition, with little belief behind it. A major exception to this was a Buddhist temple in Kamakura where Zen monks are trained. This place was literally crawling with demonic power. The difference was made by the faith put into the false religion by the trainees and their teachers. Their faith empowered the enemy to make the place a stronghold of his power. When we walked onto the grounds, our presence created immediate spiritual warfare. My wife instantly experienced an intense headache.

One major element of asserting control over the enemy is determining when he has been given permission to be in a certain place. The demons in that temple had permission to be there. For this reason, there was nothing my wife and

I could do to throw them out. We had to leave instead.

A person can give permission for a demon to hassle him without realizing what he has done. For example, on our honeymoon my wife and I went to San Diego. We visited a place that had been featured on TV a few summers before. As we went in, we had to pay a $5 cover charge each and were given cards so that we could return without paying the cover charge. A band on the stage was playing a hymn but was corrupting the words to make fun of God.

My wife immediately sensed a demonic presence in the room, invited by blasphemous music. I hoped the type of music would soon change, and I didn't want to leave. My wife's insistence became stronger and stronger until I too felt the demonic presence. We left, but a demon followed us out. I turned and rebuked it in the name of Jesus. It didn't leave. I did it again with the same result. Then I remembered the cards. We were giving the demon permission to hassle us by keeping the admission cards. I tore them up and threw them out. I then rebuked the demon, and he left.

Permission can be given to demons through keeping the wrong kinds of books, videos and music in your home. Other objects that can give demons permission are statues of false gods or items of the occult. These include crystals, Tarot cards, horoscopes, pentagrams, occult-based jewelry, Crazy-8 balls, Ouija boards, statues of dragons and wizards, and some role-playing game pieces. The demon will not leave until the objects that give him permission to stay are removed. It isn't that these items are manufactured with demons in them; it's like building houses in the park and putting up a sign saying, "Free—just move in!" The houses would soon be filled. Items dedicated to Satan by their makers, knowingly or not, invite demons to take up residence, just like houses in the park.

Chapter Six

Hearing God's Voice

The most important thing about partnering with God to perform His will is learning to hear His voice. This section deals specifically with how to develop hearing ears. Is this necessary? Can one hear God's voice without developing hearing ears? Of course. But the goal here is to be as effective as we can be in allowing God to minister through us. This cannot be done without developing hearing ears.

At one point every believer has heard God's voice, even those who think God doesn't speak in this way. Jesus said, "My sheep listen to my voice; I know them, and they follow me."[1] It must be our job to learn to hear His voice better if we really want to be used in God's service. The better we hear, the better we can obey.

How God Uses His Word in Our Lives

As stated in the section on the gift of prophecy, there are two Greek words translated "word" in our English Bibles. One word is *logos*. This means the written word. The second

Greek word is *rhema,* and it literally means the sound of the voice. It is used for a baby's cry. *Rhema* refers to a momentary word, an active word intended for a specific time and circumstance. This is the word for the voice of God we hear either directly or through others by prophecy. It is God's voice in the pastor's sermon or in a moving hymn.

Often, believers wait for long periods to hear a *rhema* word for direction. They may fail to realize that God's promise is that we are led whether or not we realize His leading. One such promise is found in Proverbs 3:6: "In all your ways acknowledge him, and he will make your paths straight." God makes our paths straight, straight toward our destiny. He doesn't lead in one direction today and in another direction tomorrow. Even when He seems to lead us through some detour, He does so to produce a needed element in our character. Our path is always straight toward increased maturity in God and toward His goal for our lives.

A second promise is found in Psalm 37:23: "If the LORD delights in a man's way, he makes his steps firm." The act of making our steps firm is not necessarily something in which we are involved. It can best be seen in retrospect, rather than in feeling His direction at every step.

Even so, God's *rhema* can direct us at critical points. Sometimes God leads us by helping us feel which direction is best for the moment; at other times we hear His voice directing us. From time to time, every committed believer is dependent upon God's *rhema* for direction.

The most important factor in hearing God's *rhema* at such times is a willingness to do whatever He asks and to go wherever He sends us. We must be willing to obey *before* we hear His direction. He will never allow us to decide to obey after hearing His direction. He requires that we trust His wisdom and His benevolent will for us. Failing to decide to go God's way, no matter what, can prevent any direction He would otherwise give. This leaves the untrusting believer wondering if God really speaks today.

Even when we are fully committed to obeying God, however, we are often dissatisfied with God's incomplete directions. We want God to lay out our lives before us. God holds our future a secret from us—and for good reason. He often sees coming hardship. If He shared that with us before preparing us for the hardship, we would worry needlessly or be frightened out of fulfilling our destiny. In God's wisdom, He made His Word (*rhema* and *logos*) "a lamp to my feet and a light to my path."[2] He provides enough light for our next step, but not much more.

God can also reveal our destiny to us. This is like seeing a city on a hill in the distance. The distance is hard to judge, but it stands out clearly. The path between you and the city is hidden. It is this high calling of which Paul wrote in Philippians 3:14: "I press on toward the goal to win the prize for which God has called me heavenward in Christ Jesus." No matter how long God takes to get us to our destiny, if we don't quit on Him, He won't quit on us. Remember Romans 11:29: "God's gifts and his call are irrevocable."

The second use of God's voice in our lives is to direct ministry. This is what has been discussed in detail in previous chapters. As we hear God's voice, we can speak with full assurance of God's will. We can speak words of faith knowing that He will act as we speak His will into existence. All of the Holy Spirit's power-tools, the gifts of the Spirit, work in this way.

THREE VOICES

There are three voices we can hear in our minds. The first and most common is the voice of our own thoughts. The second is the voice of God. His voice sounds a lot like the voice of our own thoughts, but it has a distinct character that can be recognized. Distinguishing God's voice from the voice of our own thoughts comes easier with practice. God Himself also helps us, as we will see.

The third voice is the voice of Satan, our enemy. If you know what to listen for, his voice can be recognized. To learn how, let's look at an event in the life of Elijah. The showdown on Mount Carmel had just taken place. Elijah orchestrated a mighty display of God's power and killed 450 prophets of Baal and 400 prophets of Asherah.[3] The people were led back to God, and the three and one-half years of drought were broken.

Now, the prophet is feeling depressed. He is sure Jezebel is going to hunt him down and kill him. God tells the prophet to go and stand on the mountain. God was going to pass by. As the prophet watched, a great wind came that tore the mountains apart, but God was not in the wind. Then came an earthquake, but God was not in the earthquake. After that, a fire burned through the area, but God was not in the fire. Finally, there was a still small voice.[4] By implication, God was in the voice.

Those events witnessed by Elijah are like different voices that we hear in our minds. God's voice is not like the wind—pushing, demanding, harsh. God asks, sometimes even pleads, but He never forces obedience. If you feel pushed or compelled, you are hearing the voice of Satan.

Next came the earthquake. A voice that shakes up

believers and makes them feel uneasy, nervous, or afraid is Satan's, not God's. God always brings peace and comfort even when He is challenging or rebuking us.

Then came the fire. A fiery voice is one that enflames our passions or anger. God helps us deal with passions and anger in a constructive way. When God arouses them, He does so combining it with compassion. Satan's voice motivates through base lust, passion, envy and anger.

Last came a gentle whisper. This is God's voice. God's voice is always gentle and often a whisper. This means that we must be still and quiet to hear it. Often we are too bombarded with voices vying for our attention to hear God's still, small voice. We need to learn to turn down the volume, both externally and internally, to hear God's voice consistently. We must learn to be quiet in spirit and wait for Him to speak. We must turn our attention away from the myriad of things pulling on us every moment and turn our attention to God. The very best way to do this is to worship.

Worship is not just praise to God. In praise, we are thanking God for things He has done. This is a very important thing to do. Israel was thrown into captivity more than once because they failed to be grateful to their God. How can we be treated differently if we fail to appreciate what God has done and is doing for us day by day?

Worship, however, is appreciating *who* God is rather than what He has done. It is looking up with adoration into His face and seeing His infinite love, longsuffering and kindness beyond words. Worship is thanking God for being the God He is, not the tyrant other religions worship. Worship can be all-consuming as we appreciate God's attributes one by one.

One of the reasons worship is so important in learning to hear God's voice is what it does to us. Worship puts the problems of everyday life in contrast with the Creator of the universe who loves us. The more we dwell on who God is, His power and personality, the more He frees us to see who we are in Him. He has set us free from sin.[5] He made us the head and not the tail.[6] He has given us a purpose and a destiny.[7] Worship overshadows our worries with His care. It banishes our fear through trust in His loving will. Worship puts us in the right inner posture to hear from God.

GOD'S VOICE

One thing to keep in mind about hearing God's voice is the division of responsibilities between God and us. It is God's responsibility to communicate with us so that we know it is God. Once having heard His voice, it is our responsibility to obey. If one thinks about it, there is no way we can hear God's voice unless He speaks. We cannot be sure it's God unless He helps us know. Until we are sure it is God, we cannot be held accountable for not obeying. Therefore, if someone is sincerely not sure the voice in his mind is God, he can simply ask. It is up to God to confirm it.

God confirms His voice to each one in a different way. One woman I met knew when God was speaking to her because the hair on her right forearm would stand up. As I mentioned in the section on the gift of prophecy, my teeth would tingle. Whatever way He confirms His Word, it comes with a feeling of being under the power of God. As we learn to distinguish His voice from all others, He no longer needs to pour down confirmation in ways that may seem simplistic. We can hear and obey on a more mature level.

When a new thought enters our minds at right angles to our train of thought, the new thought may be God's voice. Usually, our thoughts are connected like a train. One thought leads to another, and then to another. For instance, we might be at church and the pastor mentions family. Our thoughts jump to a son whom we have not seen for years; then to his children; then to the state of public education; then to politics; and on to a favorite president. Then we start listening to the pastor again. No matter what the path may be, our thoughts move from one topic to another with a logical connection between them. Genuine words from God break into whatever thoughts are going through our minds at the time. This is not proof that God is speaking, but it can be an indicator. A disconnected thought is a reason to look up.

God can speak to us in more ways than just in a voice. He can give us dreams while we sleep. He can give us visions, pictures seen only by our mind's eye. At times, these visions come with subtitles. He can give us impressions so we know what we *should* do. He can speak through Scripture, making a specific passage jump from the page, or He can bring a needed passage to mind. God can use all these individually or in combinations. Often, God gives me a picture with a word of prophecy. The picture more fully communicates the prophecy to me so that I can communicate it more fully to others.

CULTIVATE AN ATMOSPHERE FOR HIS WORDS

There are a number of things we can do to create an atmosphere that makes hearing God's voice easier.

Live in obedience, confession and repentance.

Nothing builds walls between God and us like sin. There are two basic concepts communicated by the New Testament words for sin. The first, usually translated as "sin," means to miss the mark or to fall short of the goal.

The second word, usually translated "transgression," means to step over the line either by deliberate action or by care-lessness. No matter how it happens, sin damages our relationship with God. It will even destroy our relationship if that sin is left unchecked.

If we are serious about hearing God's voice, we must decide to obey God's will to the full extent we understand it. To do this, we must know and understand the revealed Word of God, the Bible. We cannot live close to the edge of sinful behavior, but we must press in to the center of God's revealed will for us. We must determine to *live* as cleanly as the blood of Jesus has already made us in God's sight.

We must confess our error to God and repent when we realize that we have acted outside of God's revealed will. Repenting is more than just feeling sorry for sinning. It is deciding to change, to do things God's way rather than our own way. Even if we must repent ten times a day, when we are sincere about changing each time we repent, our repentance is acceptable to God. God then forgives us so the sin does not build a wall between God and us. God also gets involved with helping us change.

Ask God to speak.

This does two things. First, it gives God an invitation to both speak to us and help us to hear. Second, it produces an attitude of expectation within us as we wait for His voice.

Spend time worshiping.

Worship draws our attention upward to God. Our surroundings and our problems automatically fade into the background. This chapter began with a dissertation on the benefits of worship, especially when it comes to hearing

God's voice. If we want to hear God's voice on a regular basis, we must be worshippers—in church, at work, at home, everywhere we are. God desires worship to become our consistent lifestyle.

In addition to being worshiping people, praying and singing in the Spirit (tongues) is also helpful. As we flow in spiritual language, we step into the flow of the Holy Spirit Himself. It becomes easier for Him to move upon us and flow through us in other gifts of the Spirit. The combination of spiritual language and worship provides a setting for hearing God's voice. This explains why prophecy and other gifts often follow a time of corporate worship.

Don't try to "pull down" or conjure up a word from God.

Simply turn your attention to God, quiet your spirit, and wait for God to speak. He will! If God's voice seems slow in coming, keep at it. Allow God to work within you to build a greater receptivity to His voice.

FINAL CAUTIONS

Everyone can make a mistake in ministry from time to time. Test the spirits as instructed in 1 John 4:1. Make sure every prophetic word spoken over you rings true with what God is saying directly to you. Especially allow God to confirm any life-changing prophecy. The rule is to establish every word by two or three witnesses.[8] God wants you to be sure of His leading. He won't be offended if you wait for confirmation.

Also, submit to the leadership of more mature believers. They can be a real help to you in learning to hear God's voice and ministering in the power of the Holy Spirit. The role of the spiritual leader is not to make decisions for believers, but rather to provide stable direction as they grow in God. The direction of leadership must never be allowed to substitute for the direction of the Holy Spirit combined with good common sense.

Scripture is the final arbiter of all things in our lives. Make sure the word of prophecy agrees with the teaching of Scripture. If the prophecy disagrees, we must listen to and follow the Scripture.

As I mentioned earlier, I was teaching in a small meeting a long time ago when a friend asked, "Where does the Bible say that?" His question really surprised me, and I had to admit that the Scripture didn't teach what I was teaching at that moment. Those words, "Where does the Bible say that?" continue to ring in my ears every time I prepare a lesson or give a teaching.

Putting It in Shoe Leather

You now have a choice: Let the subjects in this book become just a mental exercise, or put them into practice. Using them as an exercise is easier and doesn't require much from you. Putting them into practice will place you in challenging circumstances. They will stretch you and force you to grow. There are people going to hell whom Jesus wants to rescue. There are people whom He wants to heal and set free, but He chooses to use willing believers in the process. He wants to use *you*! Without your decision to move beyond your comfort zones and let God move through you, there will be some with whom you rub elbows that He can't touch.

The best place to learn how to function in spiritual gifts is in a small group. Most sound Charismatic and Pentecostal churches encourage small groups for this purpose. There, surrounded by friends, you are in a safe environment to hear God's voice and respond to God's leading. The others in the group can encourage you and help you succeed. They can also help you avoid a danger inherent in spiritual gifts. I encourage anyone interested in growing in the gifts of the Spirit to get involved in such a group.

The danger is that if Satan can't hold you back, he will try to push you over. Satan tries to keep you from exercising spiritual gifts through fear of embarrassment. If that doesn't work, he will try to push you into over-emotionalism, thereby short-circuiting real power. Mature, stable believers can help you avoid over-emotionalism while encouraging you not to be held back by fear.

As the church began in the Book of Acts, all the gifts were fully functioning. Sometime in the first few hundred years, the Holy Spirit was repeatedly insulted and pushed aside, and the gifts fell into disuse. Through the ages there were pockets of the Holy Spirit's work, but there was no lasting move of His power. Around the turn of the twentieth century, the Holy Spirit reintroduced the gifts of the Spirit to the church. Since that time, there has been a steady recapturing of the first-century fullness. Today, we have a privilege few others in the Church Age have had. The privilege is not to just watch the Holy Spirit at work and marvel at His power, but to actually be involved in His work ourselves. Not only will our lives and churches be richer for the involvement, but the world will again be turned upside down by the power of the Spirit of God.

Notes

INTRODUCTION

1. Acts 17:29; Romans 1:20; Colossians 2:9
2. John 14:16

CHAPTER TWO
ANATOMY OF A MIRACLE

1. Matthew 4:3
2. John 5:6
3. Exodus 23:19; 34:26; Deuteronomy 14:21
4. Exodus 20:10; 31:14–15; 35:2; Leviticus 23:3; Deuteronomy 5:14
5. Matthew 23:4
6. Matthew 23:23–24
7. John 5:14
8. Romans 6:23
9. James 5:19–20
10. John 5:19
11. John 8:28; 12:49
12. John 9:1–7
13. James 4:6
14. 1 John 5:14–15
15. Greek *rhema*, lit. a spoken word

CHAPTER THREE
THE HOLY SPIRIT BAPTISM

1. John 8:31–36
2. Ephesians 1:13–14
3. Acts 1:4–8
4. John 20:22
5. Romans 8:9
6. Genesis 2:7
7. 1 Corinthians 14:14
8. 1 Corinthians 14:4
9. 1 Corinthians 14:27–28
10. 1 Corinthians 14:39
11. 2 Timothy 4:2
12. Hebrews 13:5; Deuteronomy 31:6
13. 1 John 4:8, 16
14. Genesis 6:6; 1 Samuel 15:35; Ephesians 4:30
15. Isaiah 30:18; Isaiah 40:11
16. Romans 10:9–10; 1 John 1:9
17. Acts 8:12–20

CHAPTER FOUR
THE GIFTS OF THE SPIRIT

1. 1 Corinthians 14:4
2. Romans 8:26
3. 1 Corinthians 14:2
4. 1 Corinthians 14:26–28
5. 1 Corinthians 13:1
6. 1 Corinthians 14:14–15
7. 1 Corinthians 14:18
8. 1 Corinthians 14:3
9. 1 Corinthians 14:29
10. 1 Kings 12:1–20
11. 1 Kings 16:23–24, 29

NOTES

12. 2 Kings 18:9–10
13. John 4:4
14. John 4:9
15. John 4:10
16. John 4:17–18
17. John 7:8
18. Isaiah 53:5; Matthew 8:17
19. John 2:9
20. Genesis 1:28–30
21. Mark 11:22
22. Ephesians 2:8–9

CHAPTER FIVE
SPIRITUAL WARFARE

1. Revelation 12:3–4
2. Revelation 13:8
3. Daniel 10:1–20
4. Ephesians 6:12
5. 1 Timothy 4:1, KJV
6. Acts 19:13–17
7. Matthew 8:5–10
8. John 14:9
9. Mark 9:17–29
10. Isaiah 64:6
11. Exodus 12:1–24
12. Matthew 26:28, emphasis added
13. See Ephesians 1:7; 1 John 1:7; Hebrews 9:14; 10:19
14. Ephesians 4:25–27
15. 1 John 1:9
16. Psalm 103:11–12; Micah 7:19
17. John 3:36
18. John 8:42–47

91

CHAPTER SIX
HEARING GOD'S VOICE

1. John 10:27–28
2. Psalm 119:105
3. 1 Kings 18:17–40
4. 1 Kings 19:11–12
5. Romans 6:18–22
6. Deuteronomy 28:13
7. Jeremiah 29:11
8. Deuteronomy 19:15

To contact the author:

E-mail:
 holyspiritwave@yahoo.com or
 steven.w.cole@jpl.nasa.gov

Phone:
 (626) 962–6171